ZIG AND WIKKI

in

THE COW

NADJA SPIEGELMAN & TRADE LOEFFLER

ZIG AND WIKKI

in

THE COW

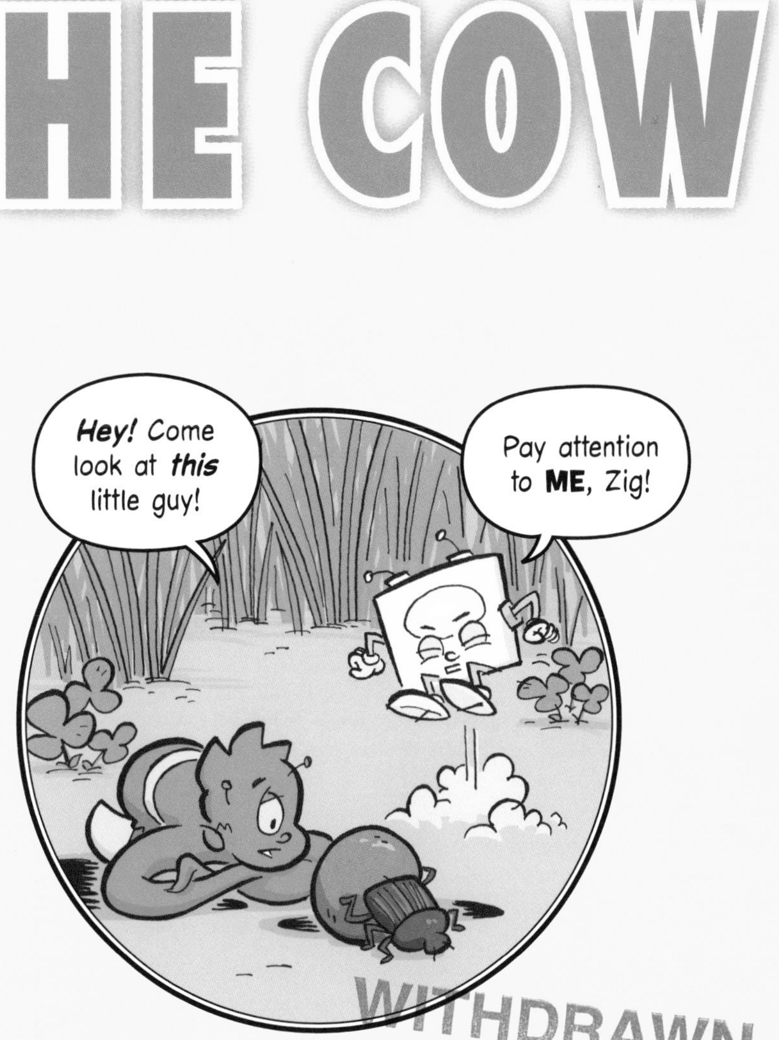
Hey! Come look at this little guy!
Pay attention to ME, Zig!

A TOON BOOK BY

NADJA SPIEGELMAN & TRADE LOEFFLER

TOON BOOKS IS AN IMPRINT OF CANDLEWICK PRESS

For Dash *−Nadja*

For Annalisa, Clark, and Boo *−Trade*

Editorial Director: FRANÇOISE MOULY

Book Design: FRANÇOISE MOULY & JONATHAN BENNETT

Guest Editor: GEOFFREY HAYES

Wikki's Screen Drawings: MYKEN BOMBERGER

TRADE LOEFFLER'S artwork was drawn in black ink on paper and colored digitally

A TOON Book™ © 2012 RAW Junior, LLC, 27 Greene Street, New York, NY 10013. TOON Books® is an imprint of Candlewick Press, 99 Dover Street, Somerville, MA 02144. No part of this book may be used or reproduced in any manner whatsoever without written permission except in the case of brief quotations embodied in critical articles and reviews. All photos used by permission. Page 8: © Igor Burchenkov / iStockphoto.com; Page 16: © 2011 Kyle Slade; Page 19: © Zralok / Dreamstime.com; Page 20: © Shariffc / Dreamstime.com; Page 21: © Vlue / Dreamstime.com; Page 33: Slides © Mel Yokoyama; Page 40: Cow mouth © 2011 Keven Law (http://www.flickr.com/photos/kevenlaw/), Cow tongue © Kurt / Dreamstime.com, Cow nose © 2011 Jessica Warren; BACK COVER: Cow © Tilo / Dreamstime.com. TOON Books®, LITTLE LIT® and TOON Into Reading™ are trademarks of RAW Junior, LLC. All rights reserved. Printed in Singapore by Tien Wah Press (Pte.) Ltd.

Library of Congress Cataloging-in-Publication Data:

Spiegelman, Nadja.

Zig and Wikki in The cow : a TOON book / by Nadja Spiegelman & [illustrated by] Trade Loeffler.

p. cm.

Summary: Two extraterrestrial friends land on Earth in the center of a farm ecosystem, where an argument forces them to separate, only to be brought back together in the stomach of a cow.

ISBN 978-1-935179-15-3 (hardcover)

1. Graphic novels. [1. Graphic novels. 2. Extraterrestrial beings–Fiction. 3. Farms–Fiction. 4. Flies–Fiction.] I. Loeffler, Trade, ill. II. Title. III. Title: Cow.

PZ7.7.S65Zj 2012   741.5'973–dc23   2011026676

ISBN 13: 978-1-935179-15-3 ISBN 10: 1-935179-15-2

12 13 14 15 16 17 TWP 10 9 8 7 6 5 4 3 2 1

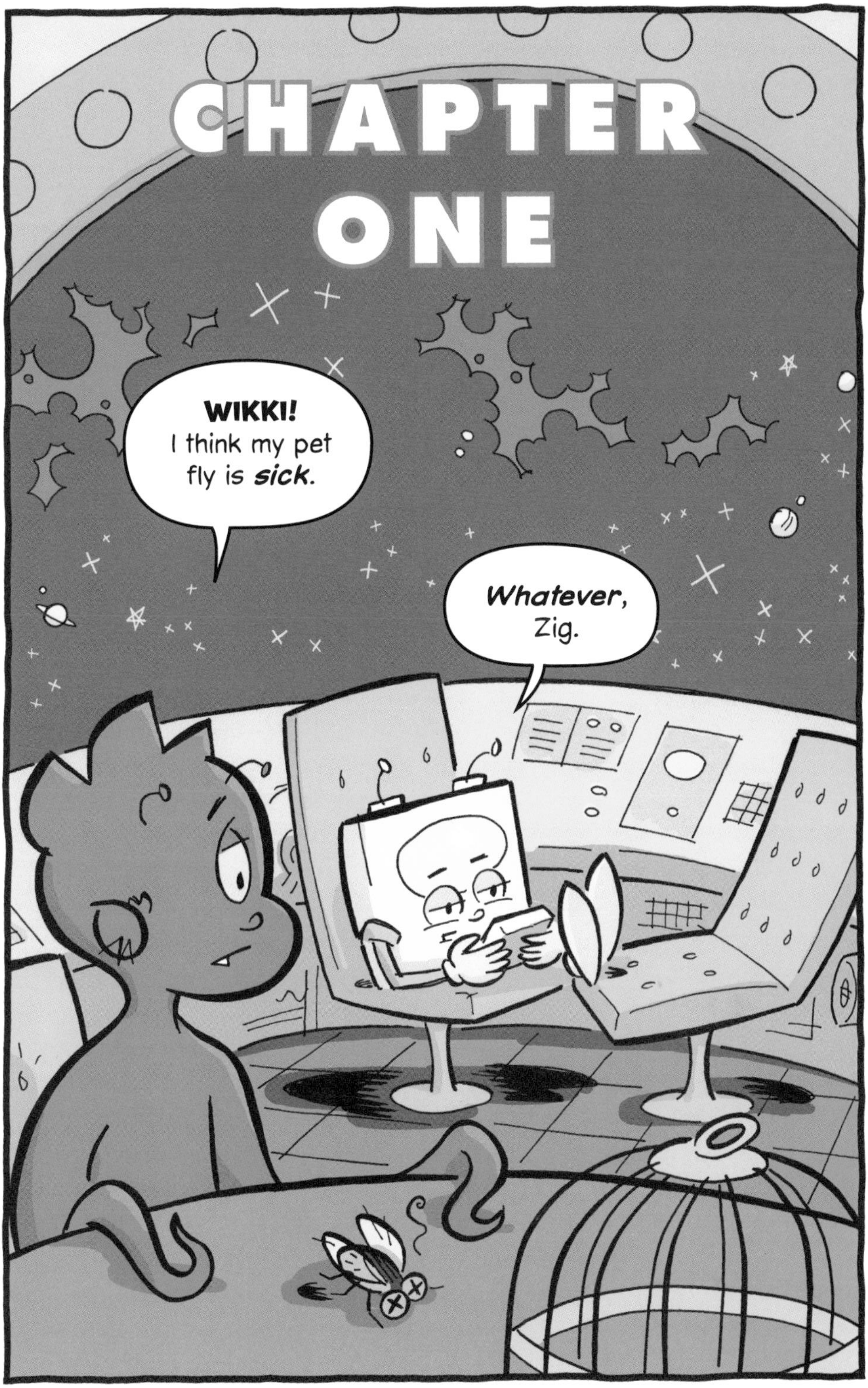
CHAPTER ONE
WIKKI! I think my pet fly is ***sick.***
Whatever, Zig.

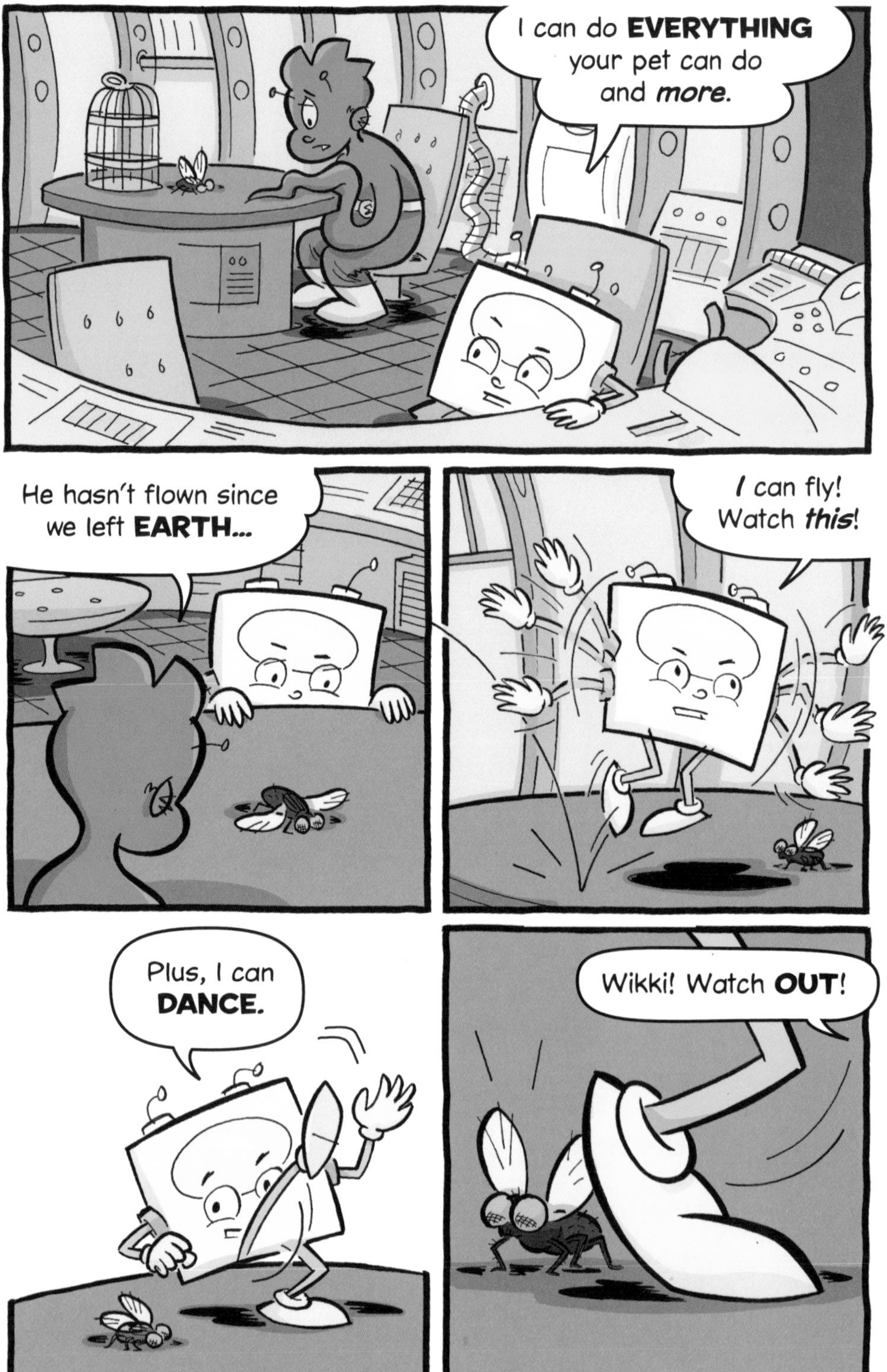
I can do **EVERYTHING** your pet can do and *more.*
He hasn't flown since we left **EARTH...**
I can fly! Watch *this*!
Plus, I can **DANCE.**
Wikki! Watch **OUT**!

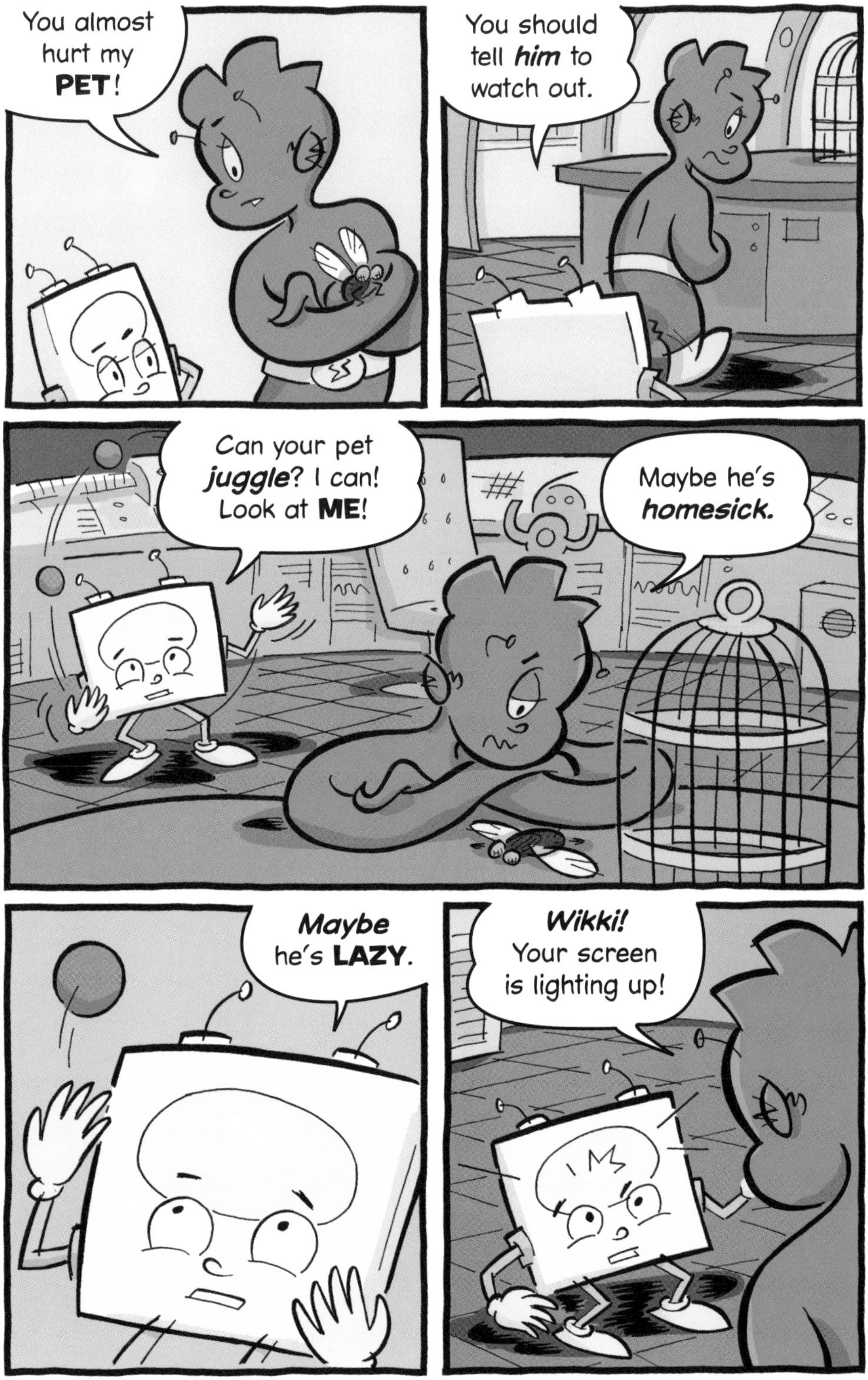
You almost hurt my **PET**!
You should tell ***him*** to watch out.
Can your pet ***juggle***? I can! Look at **ME**!
Maybe he's ***homesick.***
Maybe he's **LAZY**.
Wikki! Your screen is lighting up!

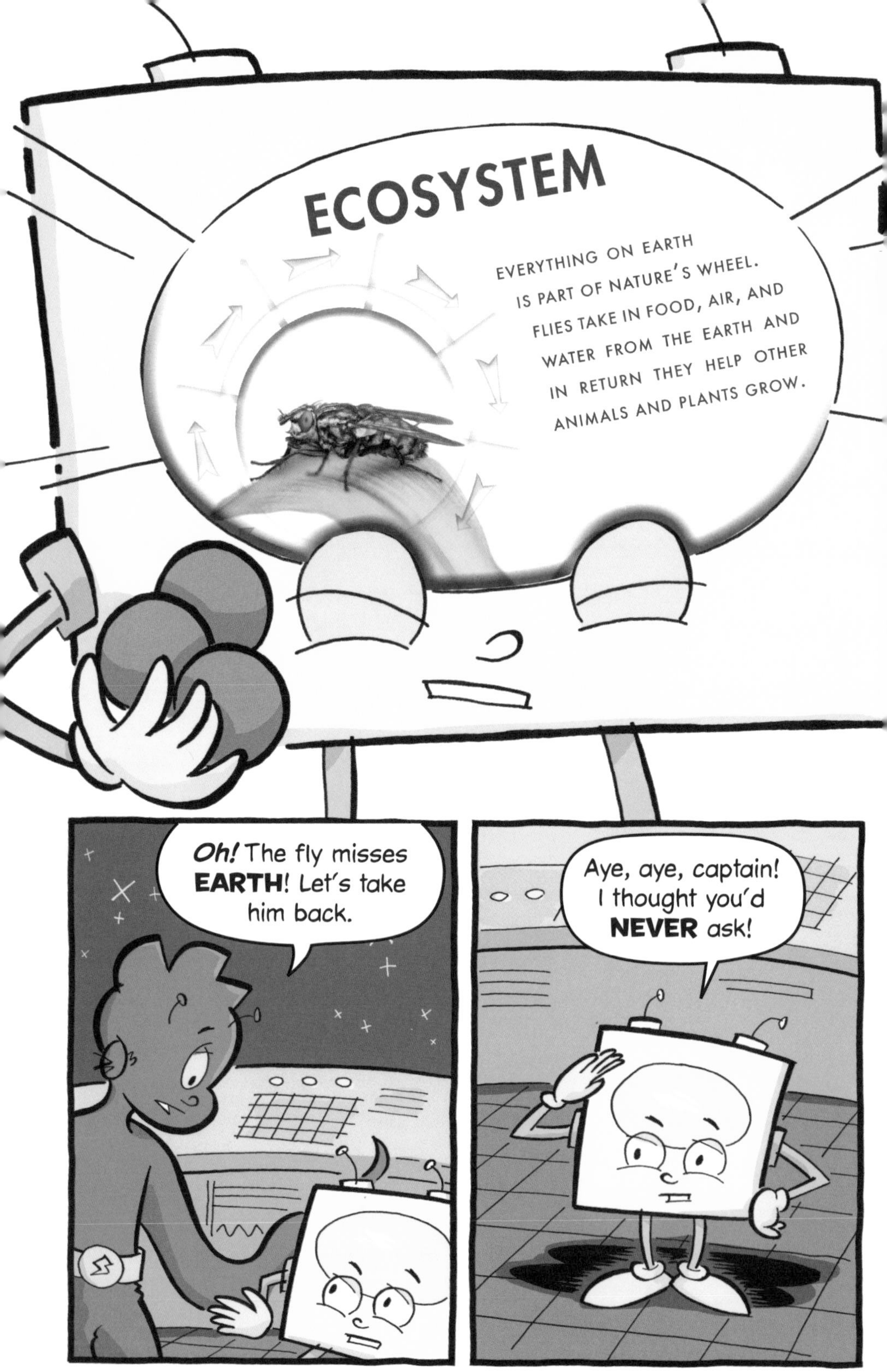
ECOSYSTEM
EVERYTHING ON EARTH IS PART OF NATURE'S WHEEL. FLIES TAKE IN FOOD, AIR, AND WATER FROM THE EARTH AND IN RETURN THEY HELP OTHER ANIMALS AND PLANTS GROW.
Oh! The fly misses EARTH! Let's take him back.
Aye, aye, captain! I thought you'd NEVER ask!

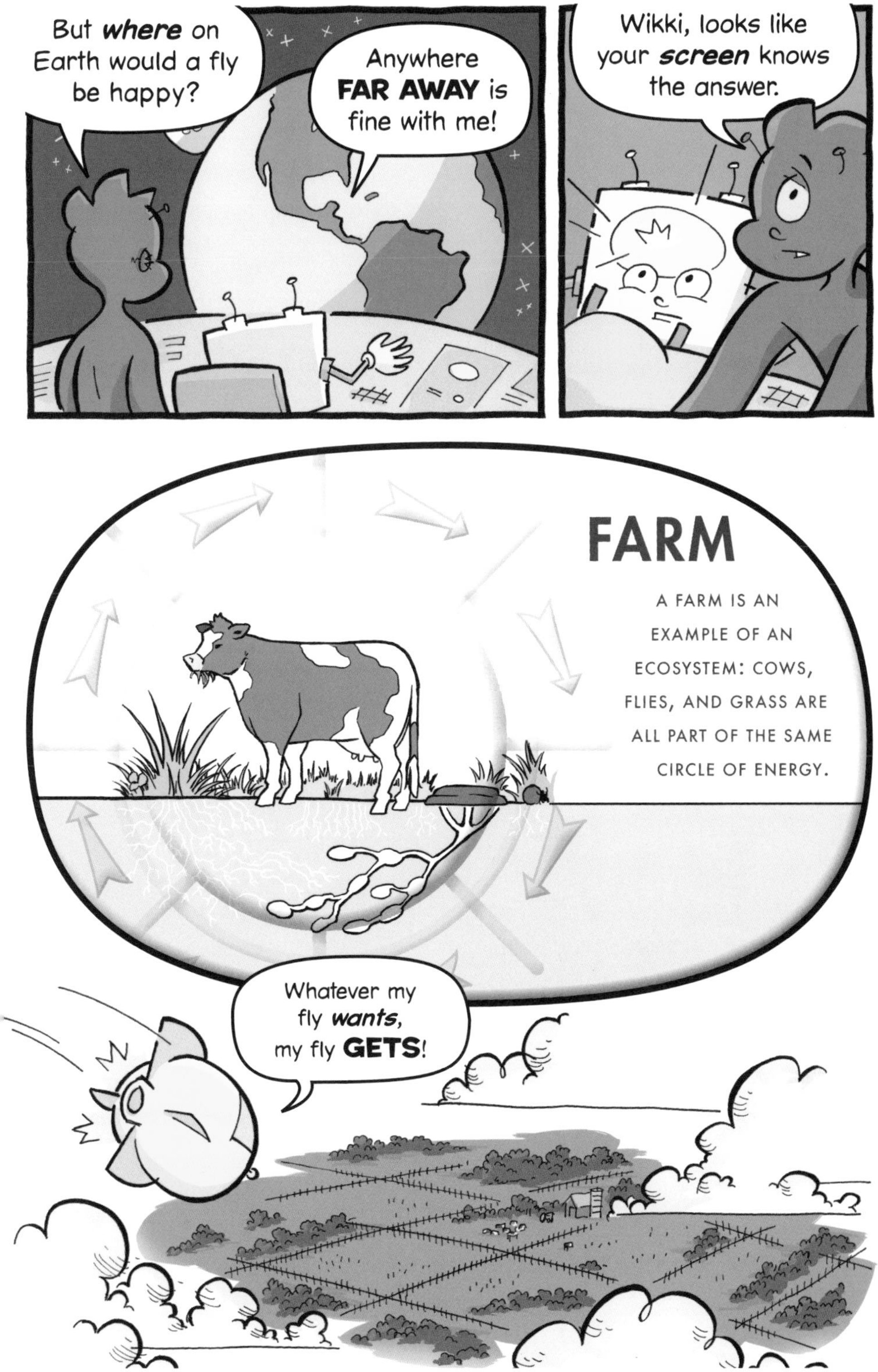

But *where* on Earth would a fly be happy?
Anywhere **FAR AWAY** is fine with me!
Wikki, looks like your *screen* knows the answer.
FARM
A FARM IS AN EXAMPLE OF AN ECOSYSTEM: COWS, FLIES, AND GRASS ARE ALL PART OF THE SAME CIRCLE OF ENERGY.
Whatever my fly *wants*, my fly **GETS**!

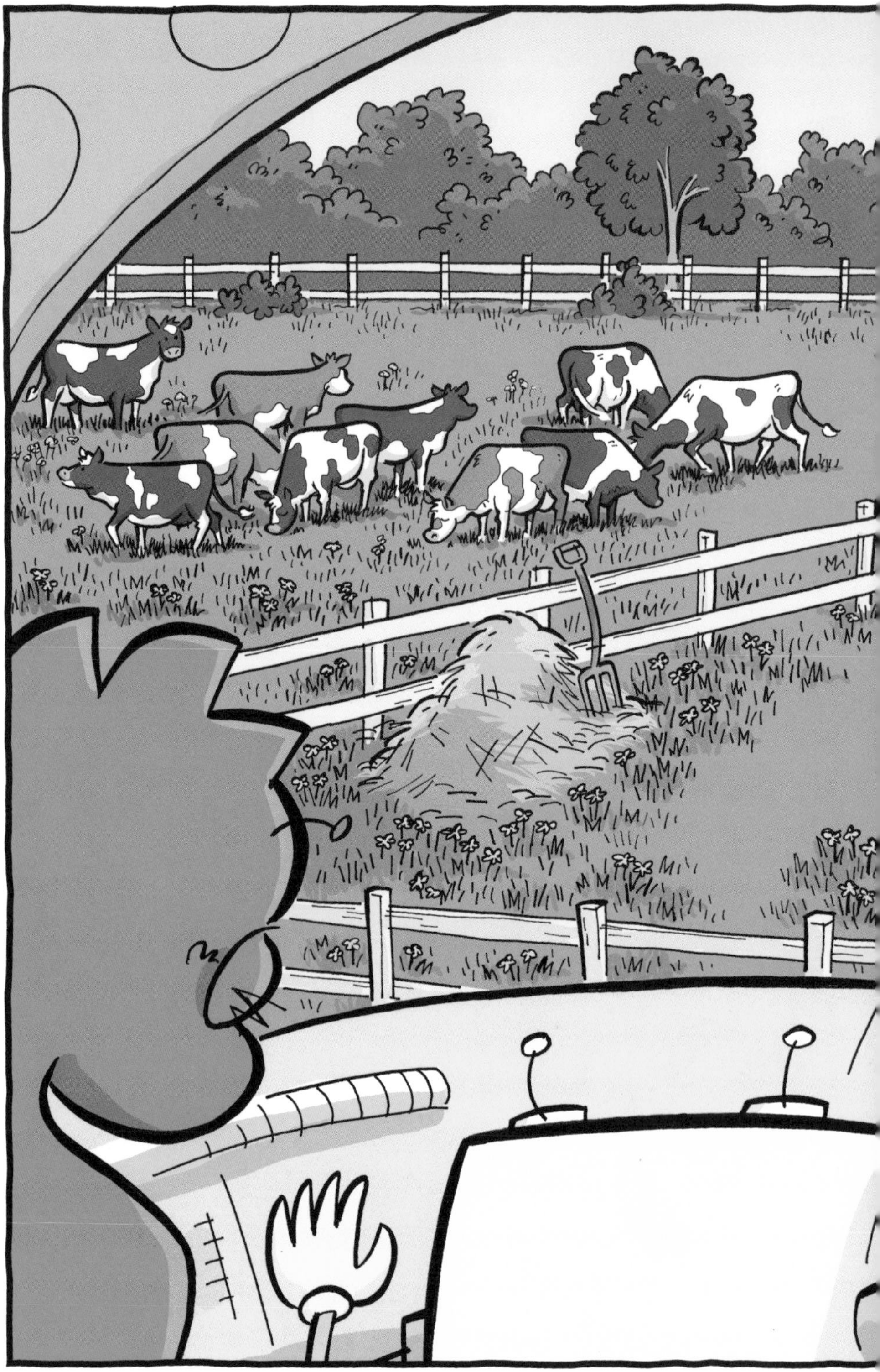

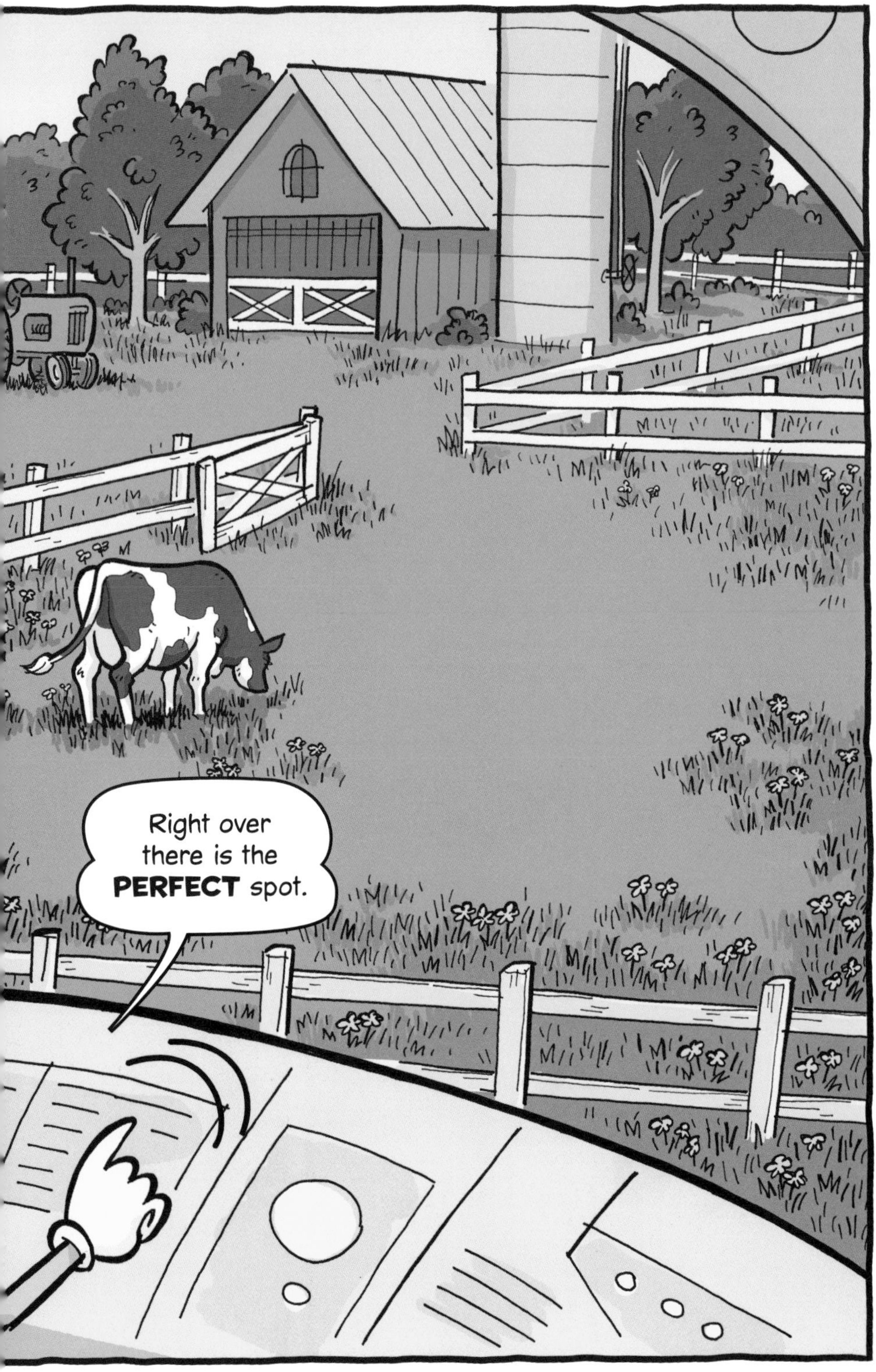
Right over there is the **PERFECT** spot.

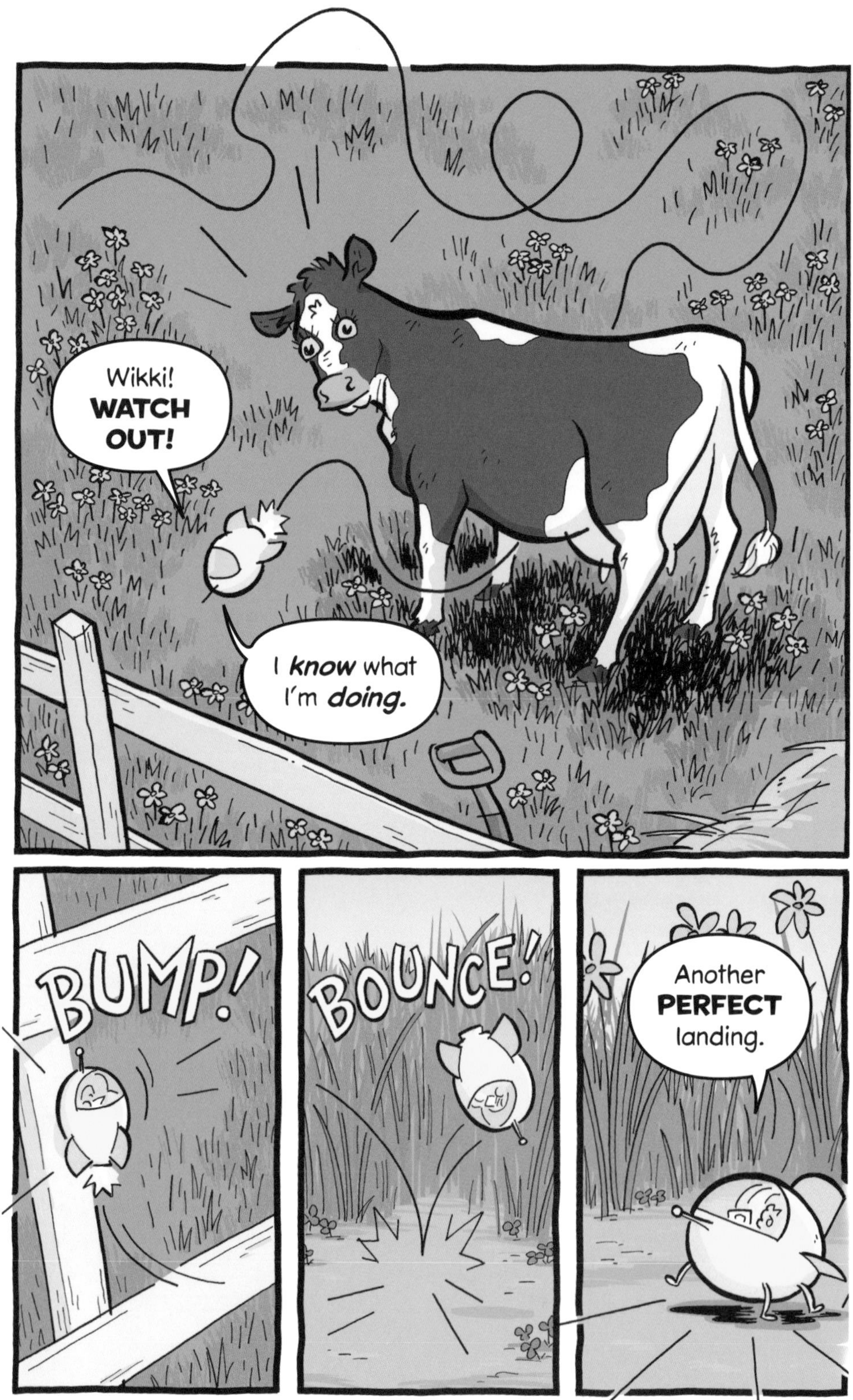

Wikki! WATCH OUT!
I know what I'm doing.
BUMP!
BOUNCE!
Another PERFECT landing.

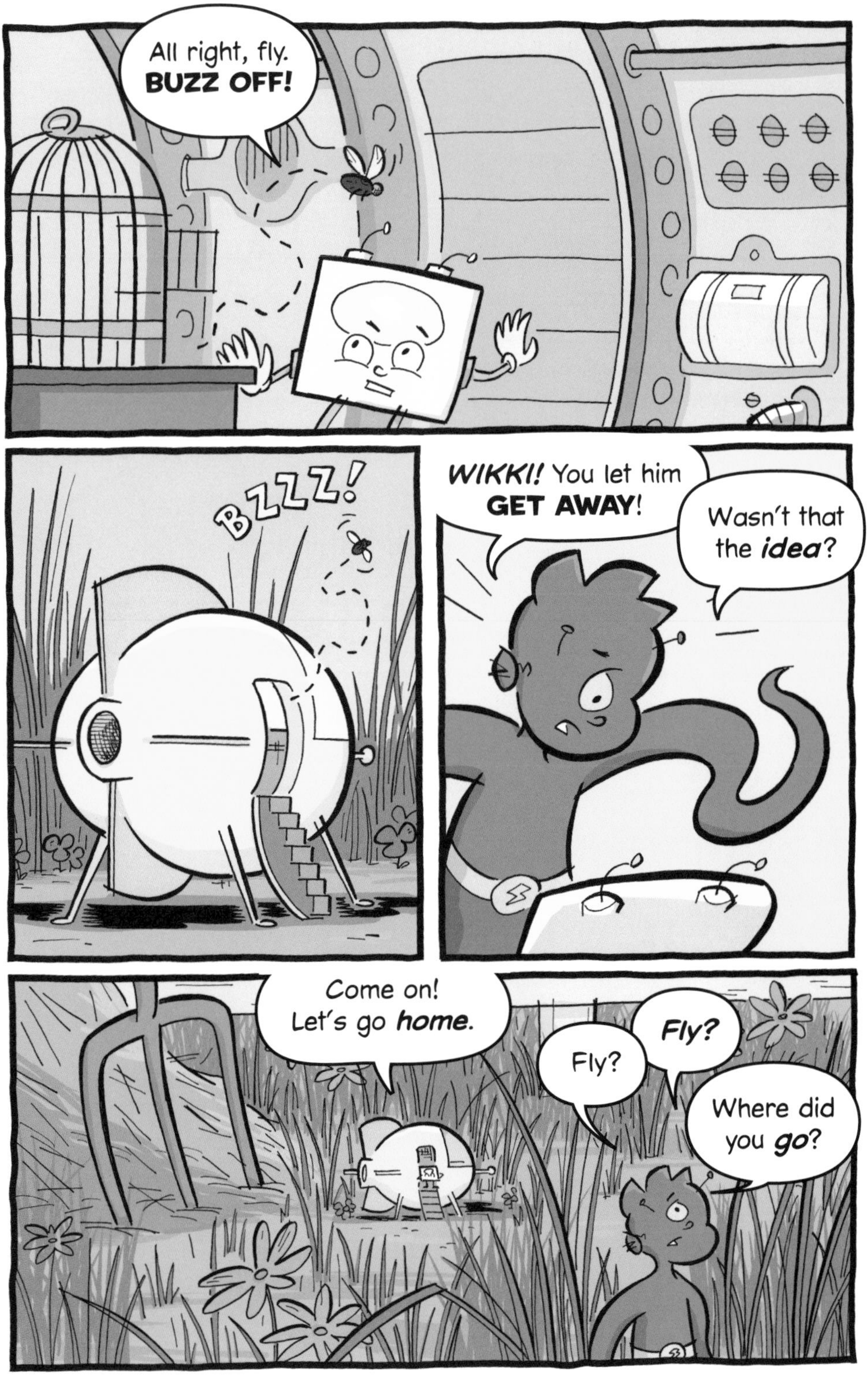
All right, fly.
BUZZ OFF!
BZZZ!
WIKKI! You let him **GET AWAY**!
Wasn't that the ***idea***?
Come on! Let's go ***home***.
Fly?
Fly?
Where did you ***go***?

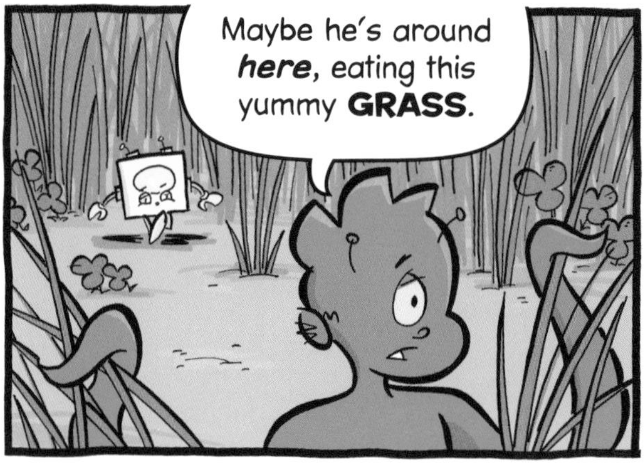
Maybe he's around *here*, eating this yummy **GRASS**.

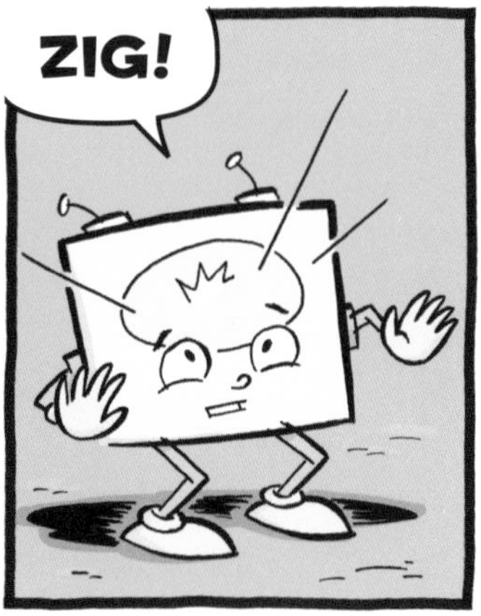
ZIG!

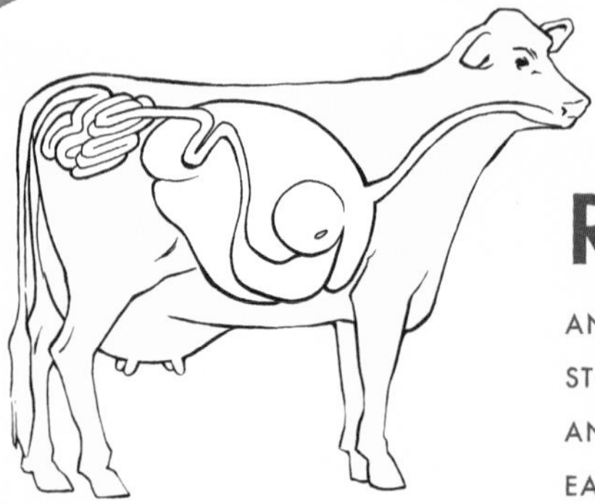

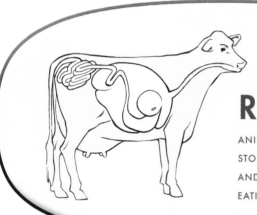

RUMINANTS

ANIMALS WHO HAVE SPECIAL STOMACHS, LIKE COWS, GOATS AND DEER, CAN GET ENERGY FROM EATING GRASS.

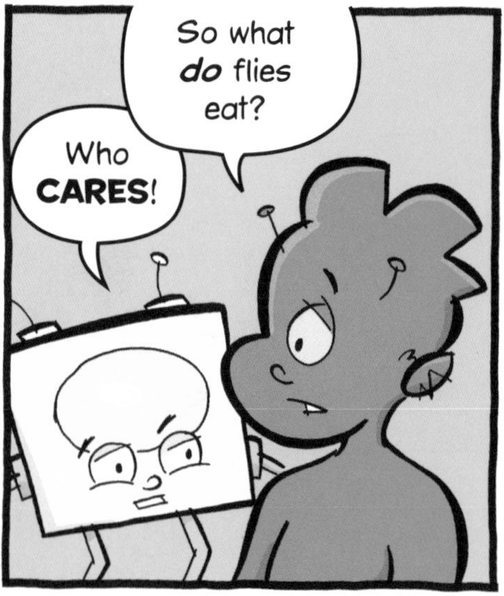
So what *do* flies eat?
Who **CARES**!

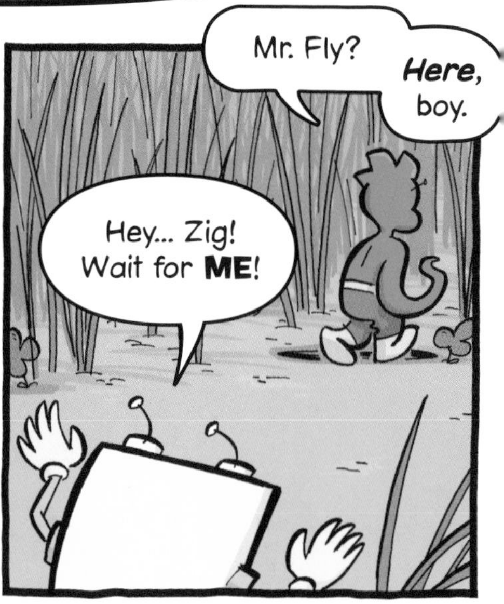
Mr. Fly?
Here, boy.
Hey... Zig! Wait for **ME**!

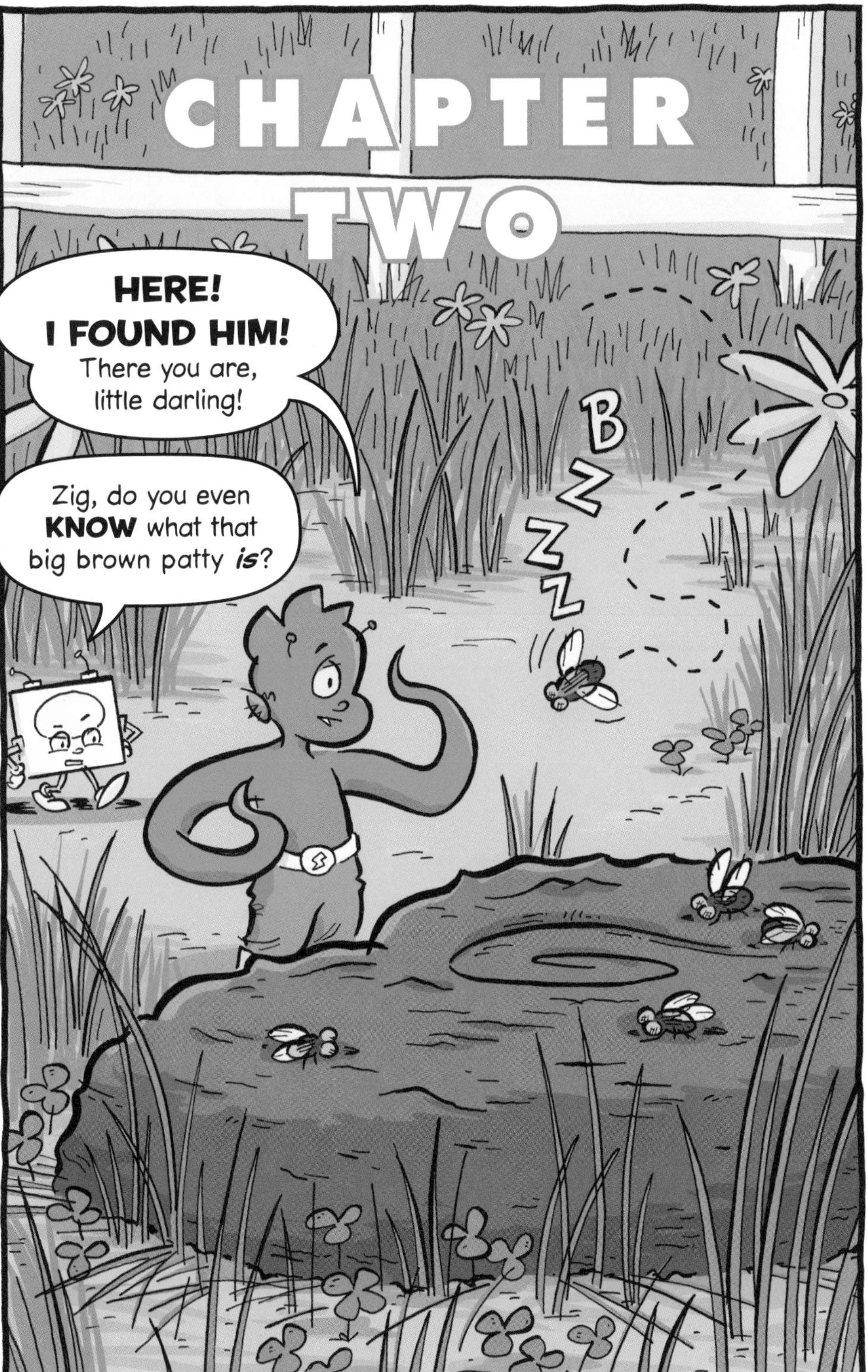

CHAPTER TWO
HERE! I FOUND HIM! There you are, little darling!
Zig, do you even **KNOW** what that big brown patty *is*?
BZZZ

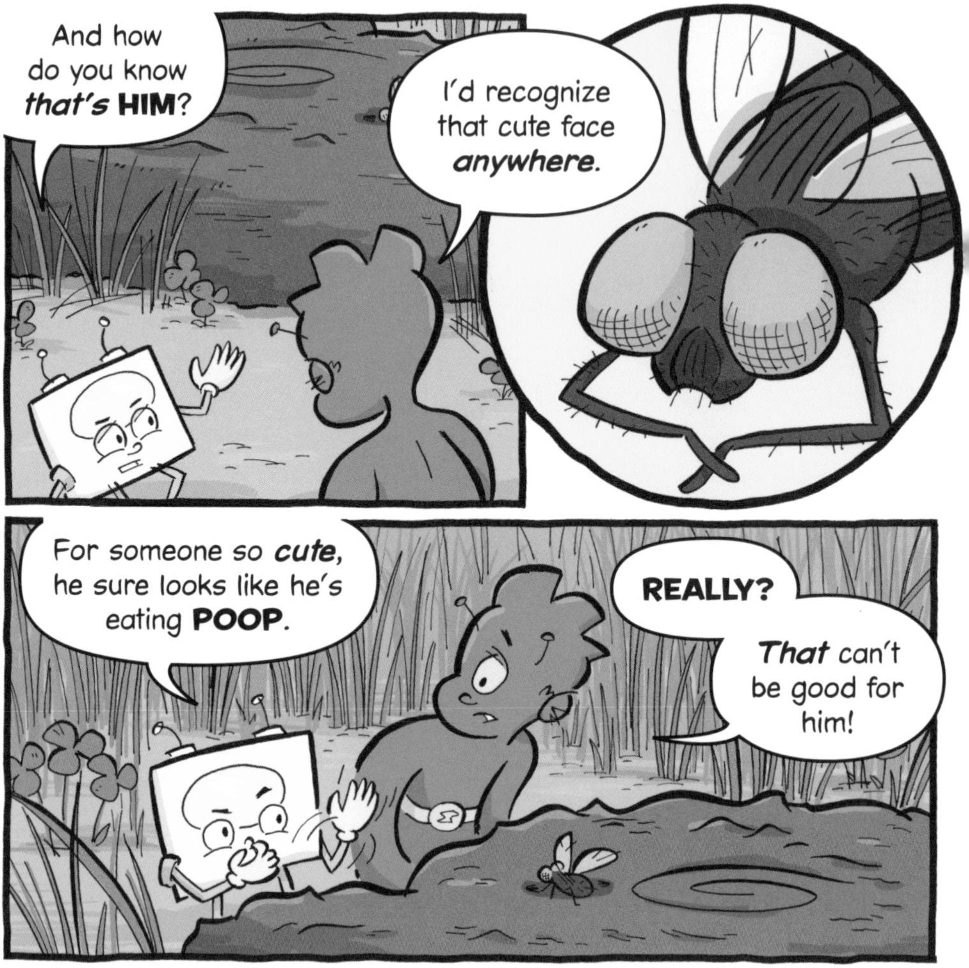
And how do you know *that's* **HIM**?
I'd recognize that cute face *anywhere.*
For someone so *cute*, he sure looks like he's eating **POOP**.
REALLY?
That can't be good for him!

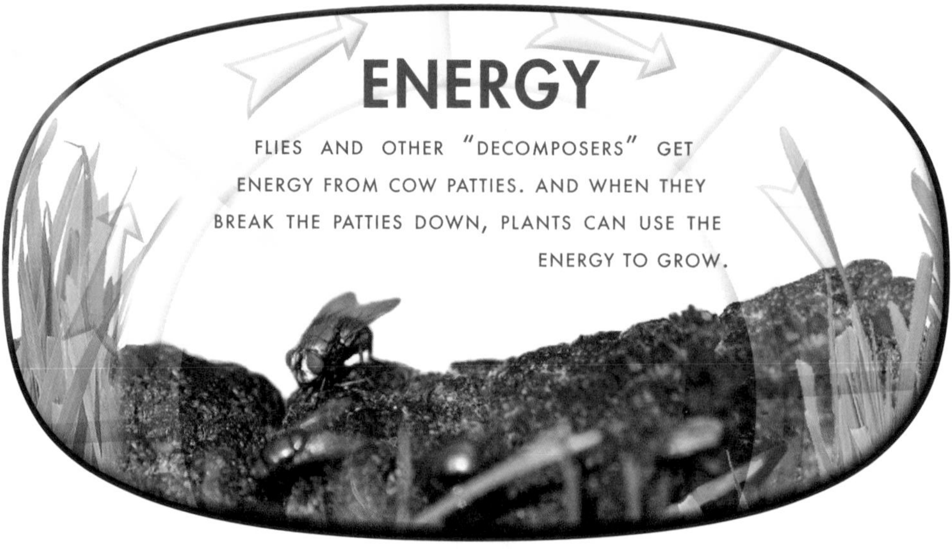

ENERGY

FLIES AND OTHER "DECOMPOSERS" GET ENERGY FROM COW PATTIES. AND WHEN THEY BREAK THE PATTIES DOWN, PLANTS CAN USE THE ENERGY TO GROW.

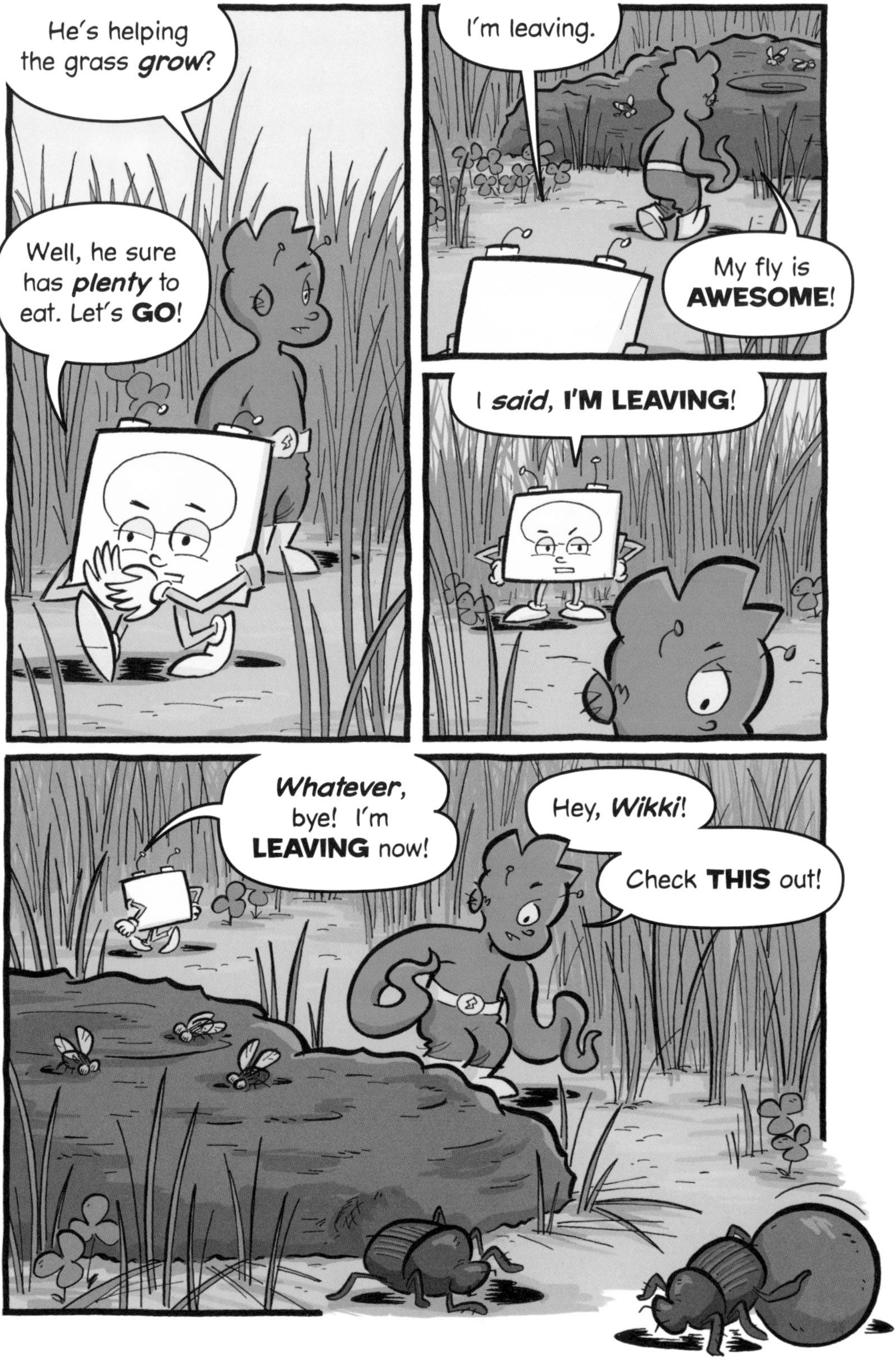
He's helping the grass *grow*?
Well, he sure has *plenty* to eat. Let's **GO**!
I'm leaving.
My fly is **AWESOME**!
I *said*, **I'M LEAVING**!
Whatever, bye! I'm **LEAVING** now!
Hey, *Wikki*!
Check **THIS** out!

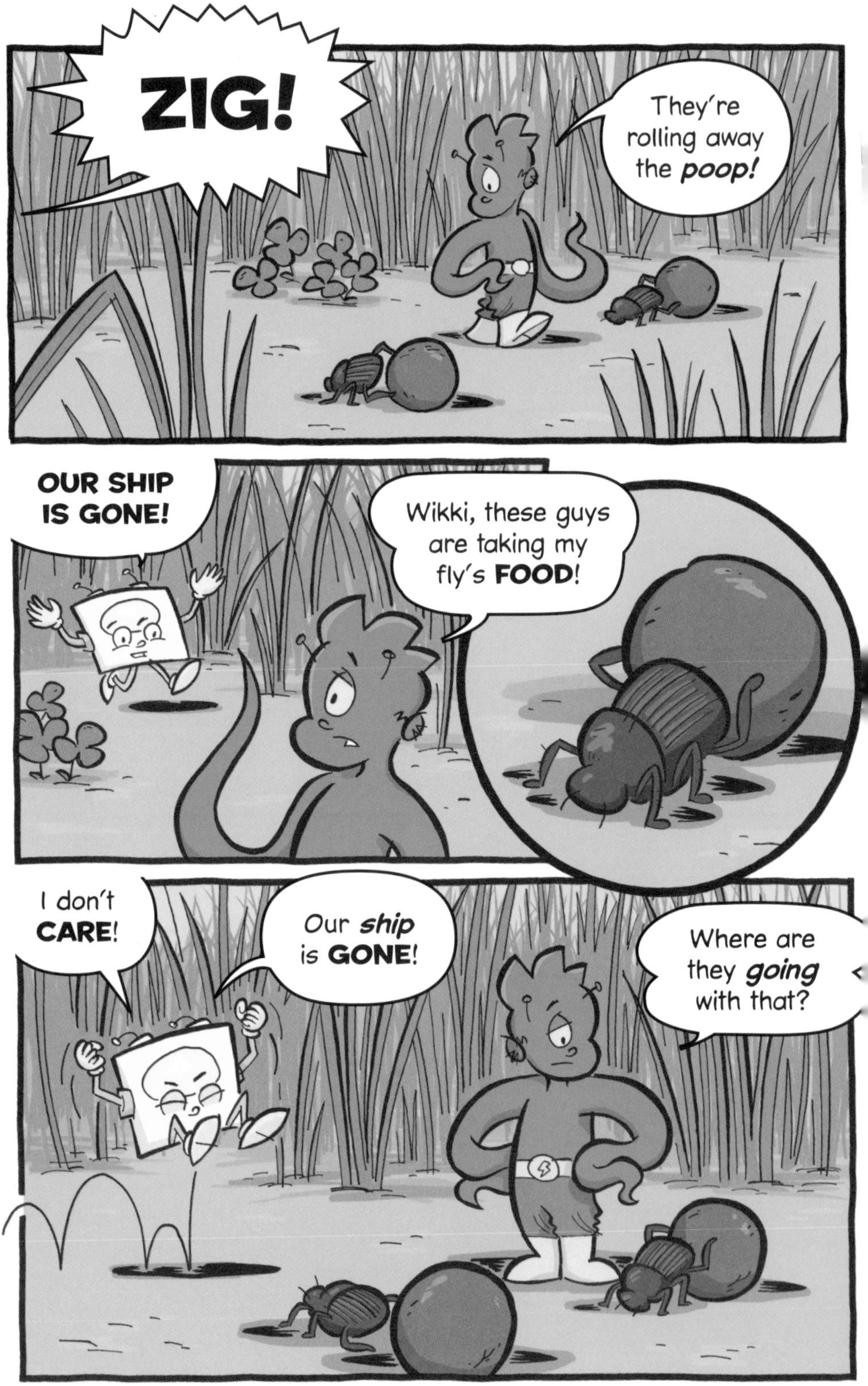
ZIG!
They're rolling away the **poop!**
OUR SHIP IS GONE!
Wikki, these guys are taking my fly's **FOOD**!
I don't **CARE**!
Our ***ship*** is **GONE**!
Where are they ***going*** with that?

DUNG BEETLES

THERE ARE THREE TYPES OF DUNG BEETLES: *ROLLERS* ROLL BALLS OF DUNG AWAY TO BURY UNDERGROUND, *DWELLERS* LIVE IN THE DUNG, AND *TUNNELERS* BUILD TUNNELS IN THE SOIL.

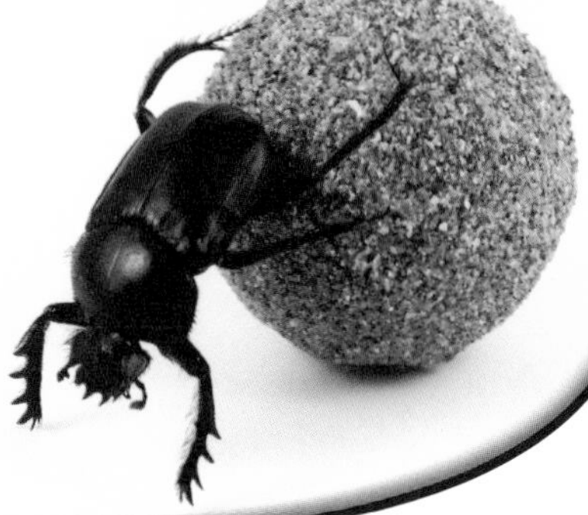

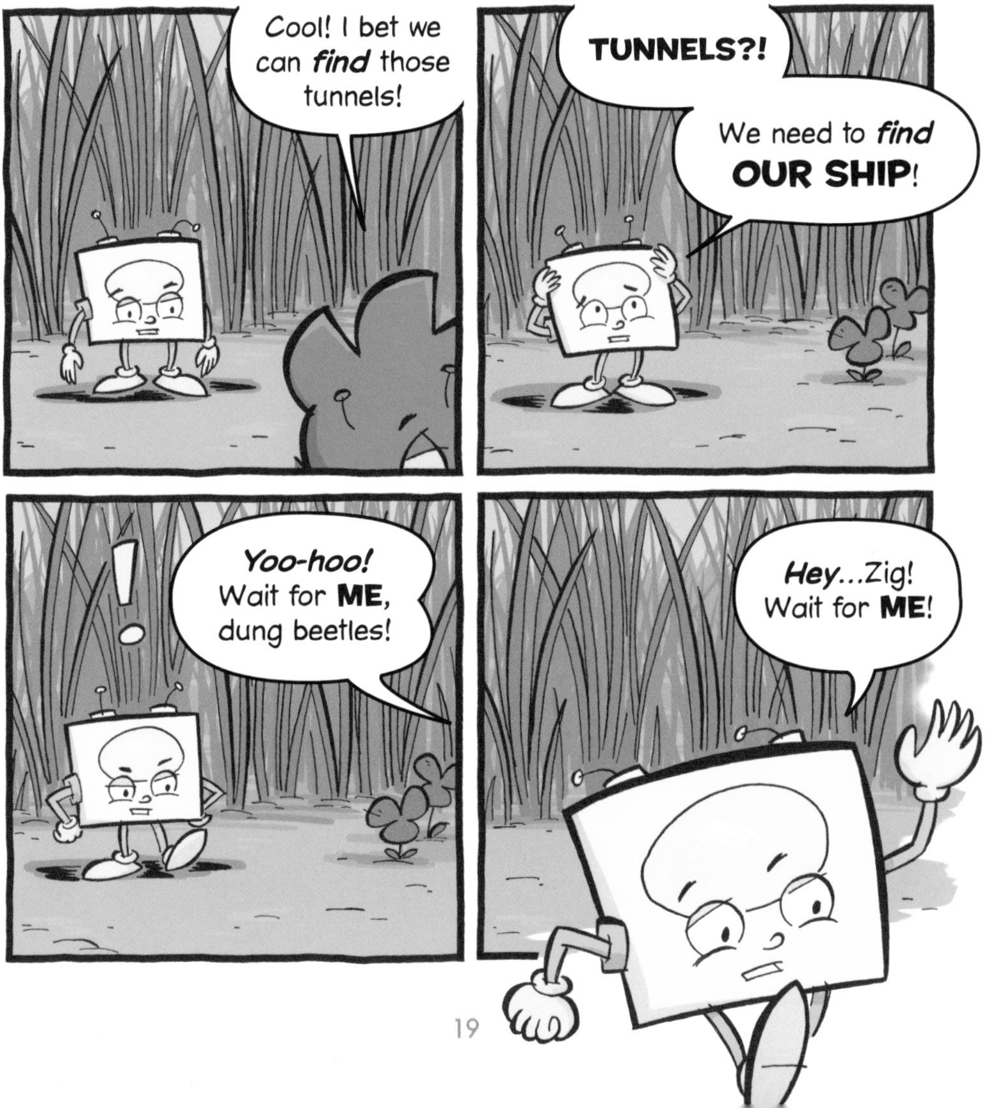
Cool! I bet we can *find* those tunnels!
TUNNELS?!
We need to *find* **OUR SHIP**!
!
Yoo-hoo! Wait for **ME**, dung beetles!
Hey...Zig! Wait for **ME**!

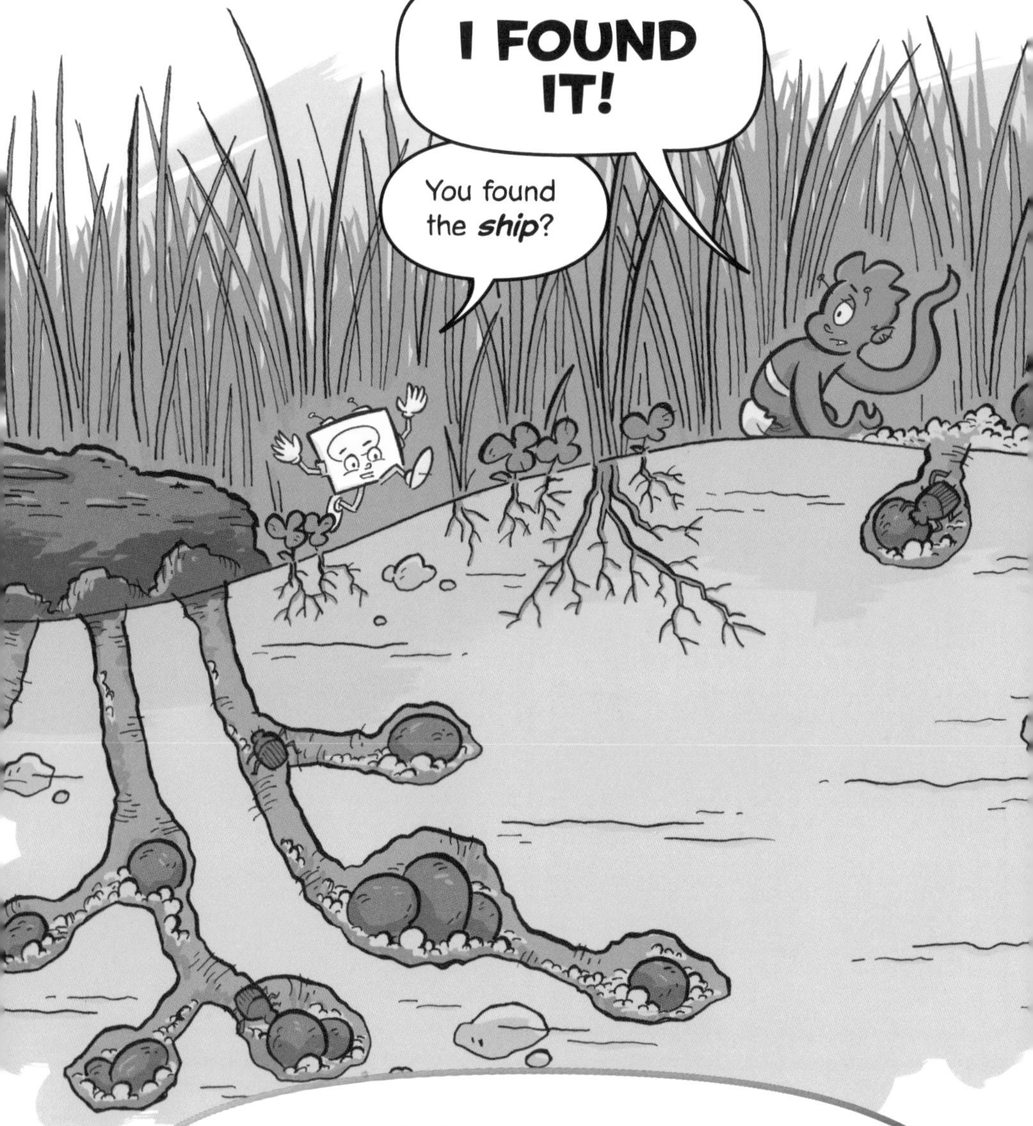
I FOUND IT!
You found the *ship*?

DECOMPOSERS

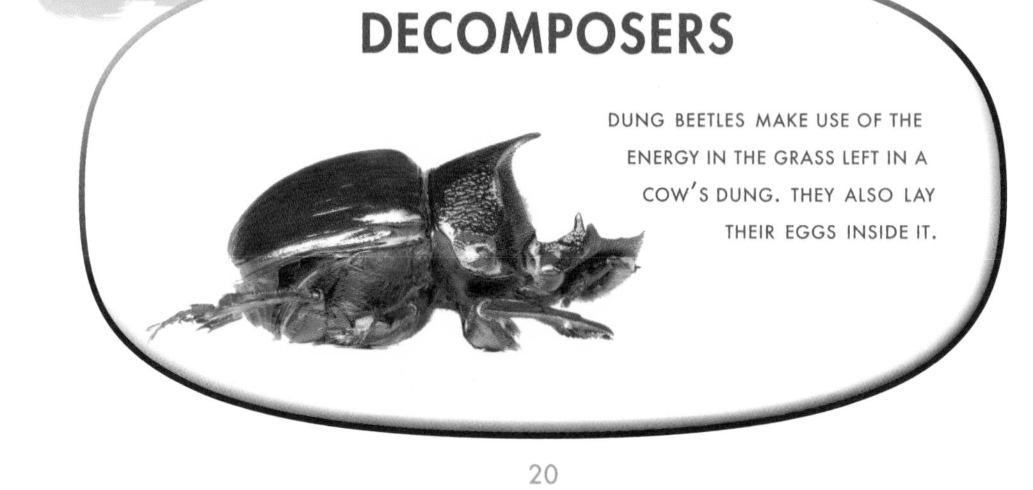

DUNG BEETLES MAKE USE OF THE ENERGY IN THE GRASS LEFT IN A COW'S DUNG. THEY ALSO LAY THEIR EGGS INSIDE IT.

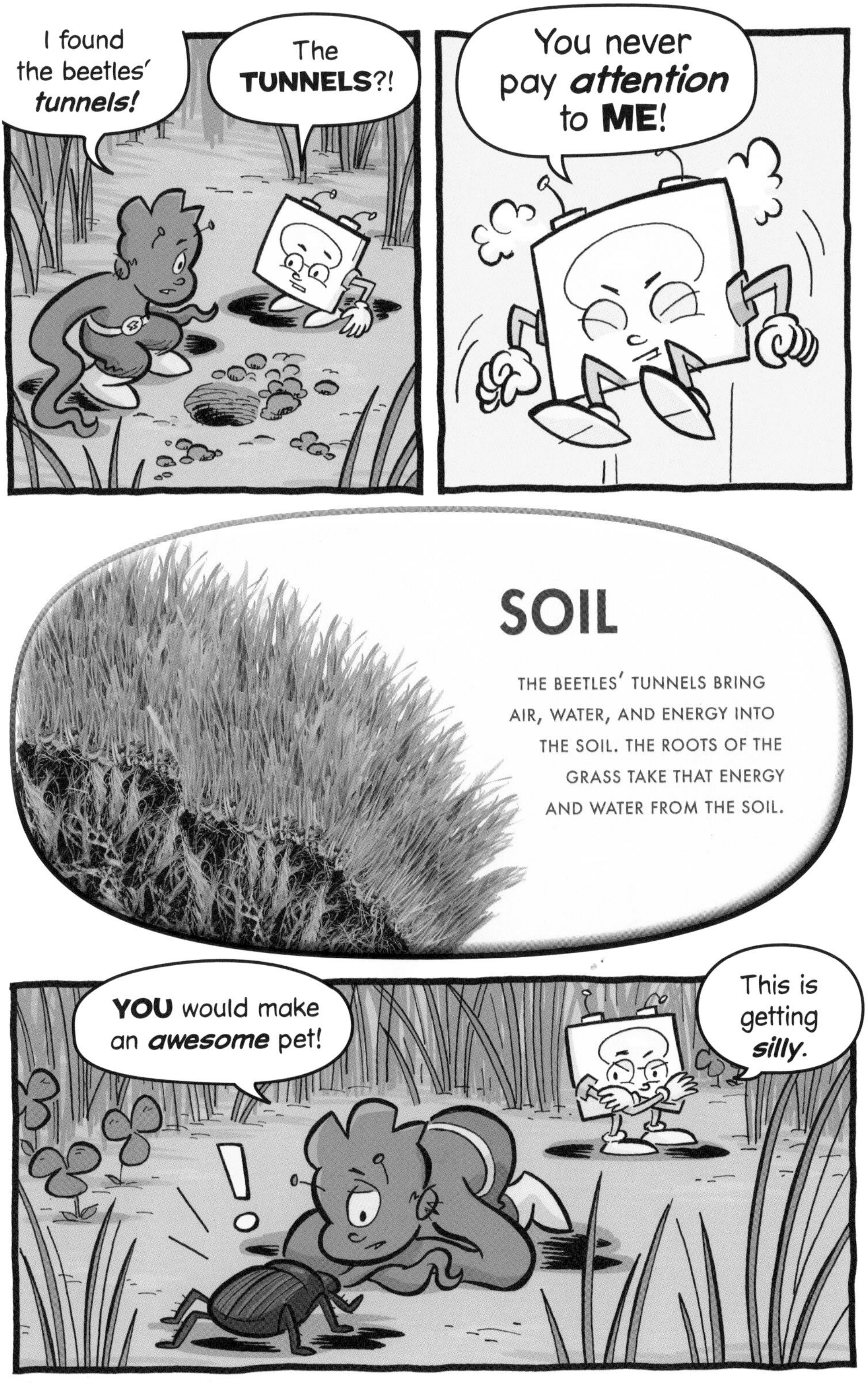
I found the beetles' *tunnels!*
The **TUNNELS**?!
You never pay ***attention*** to **ME**!
SOIL
THE BEETLES' TUNNELS BRING AIR, WATER, AND ENERGY INTO THE SOIL. THE ROOTS OF THE GRASS TAKE THAT ENERGY AND WATER FROM THE SOIL.
YOU would make an ***awesome*** pet!
This is getting *silly*.

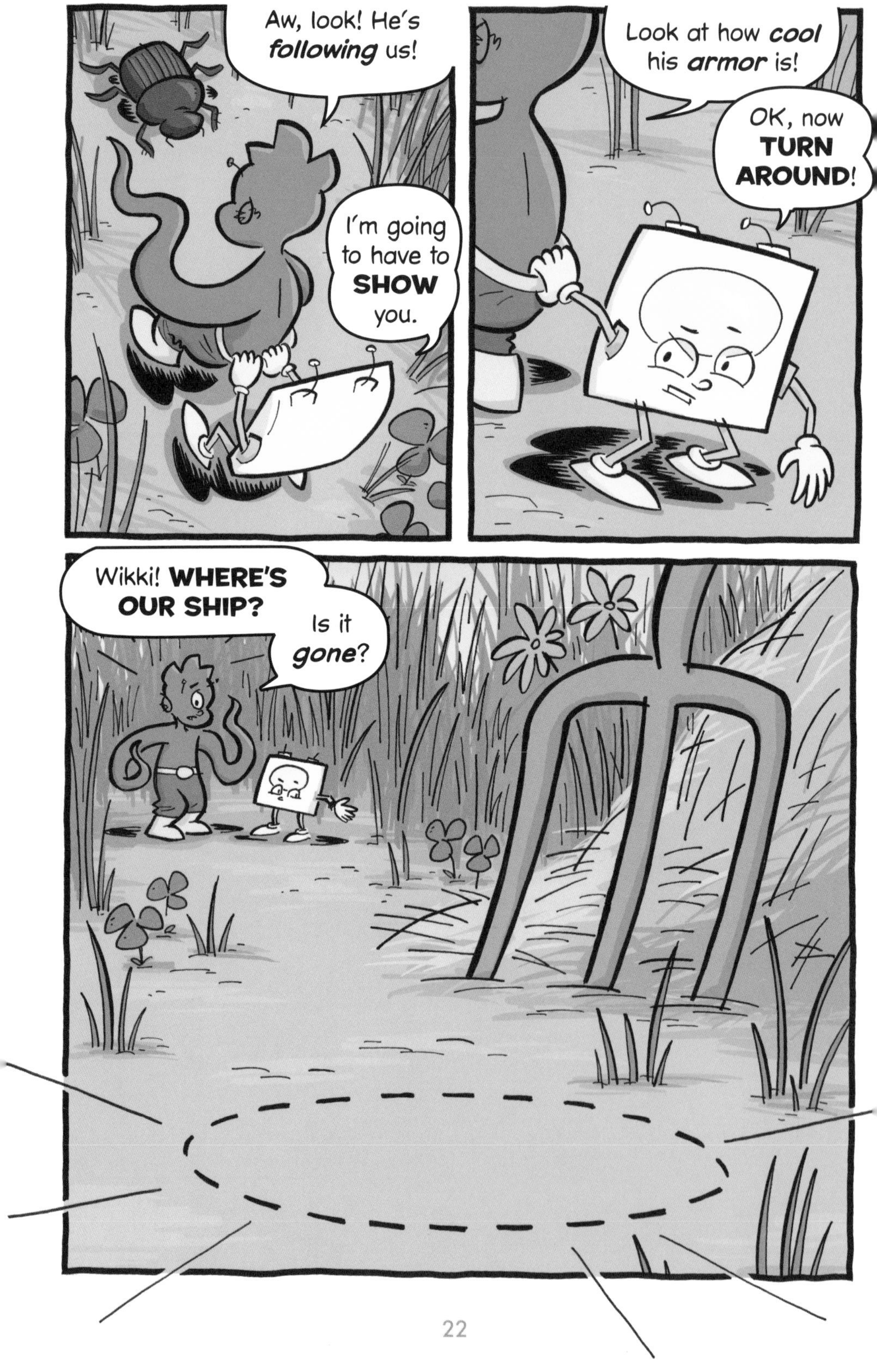
Aw, look! He's *following* us!
I'm going to have to **SHOW** you.
Look at how *cool* his *armor* is!
OK, now **TURN AROUND**!
Wikki! **WHERE'S OUR SHIP?**
Is it *gone*?

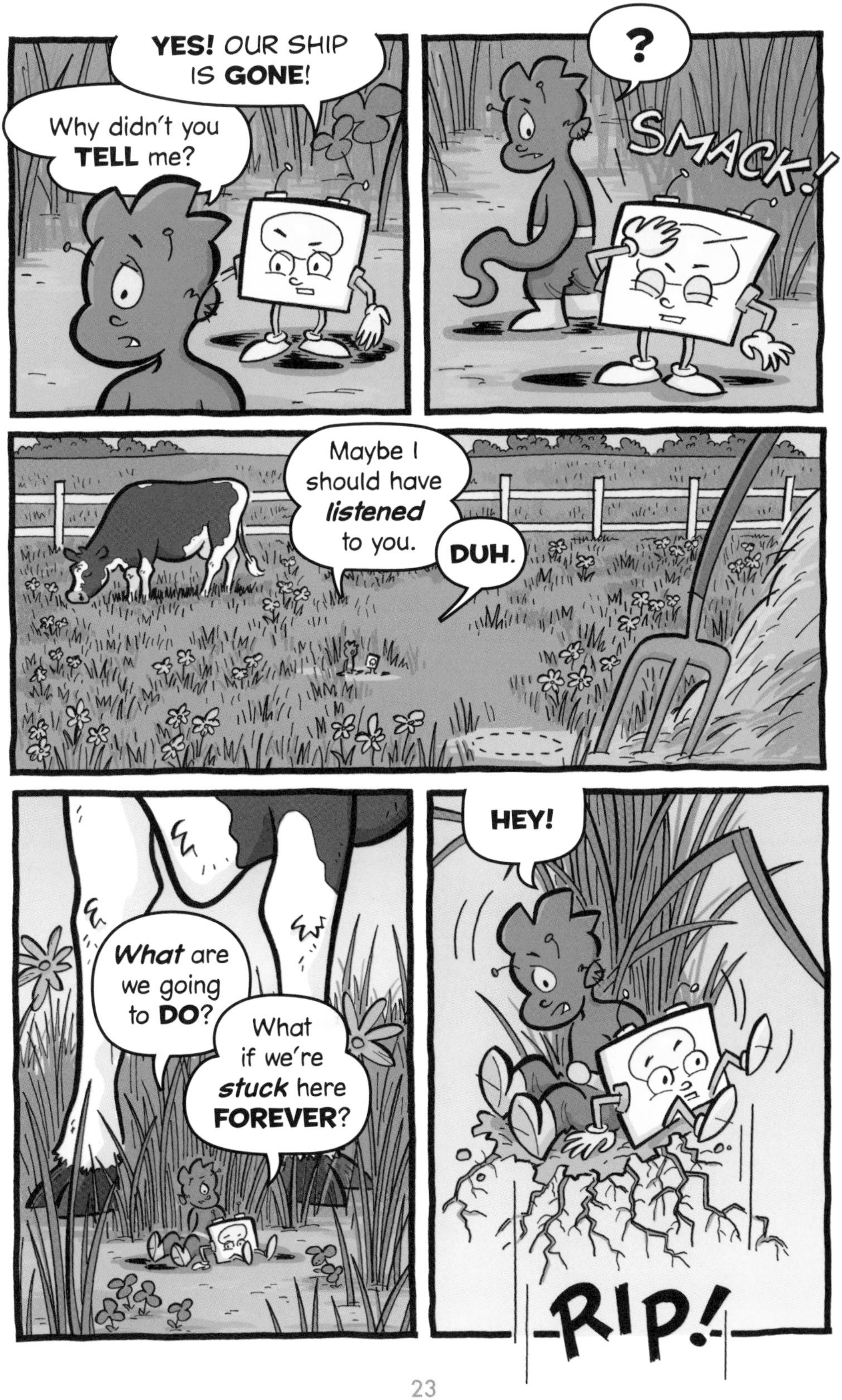

YES! OUR SHIP IS GONE!
Why didn't you TELL me?
?
SMACK!
Maybe I should have listened to you.
DUH.
What are we going to DO?
What if we're stuck here FOREVER?
HEY!
RIP!

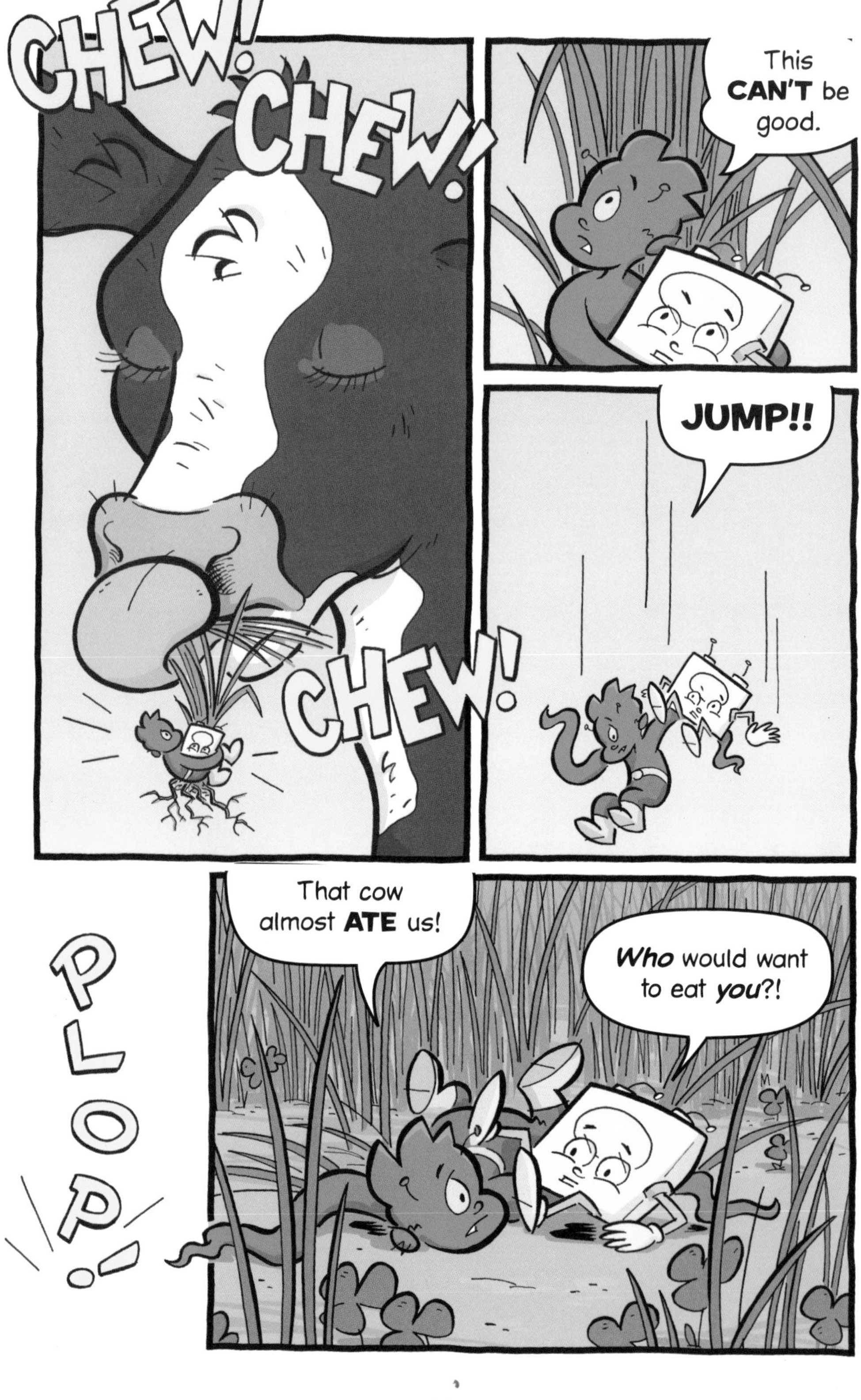
CHEW! CHEW!
This CAN'T be good.
JUMP!!
CHEW!
That cow almost ATE us!
Who would want to eat you?!
PLOP!

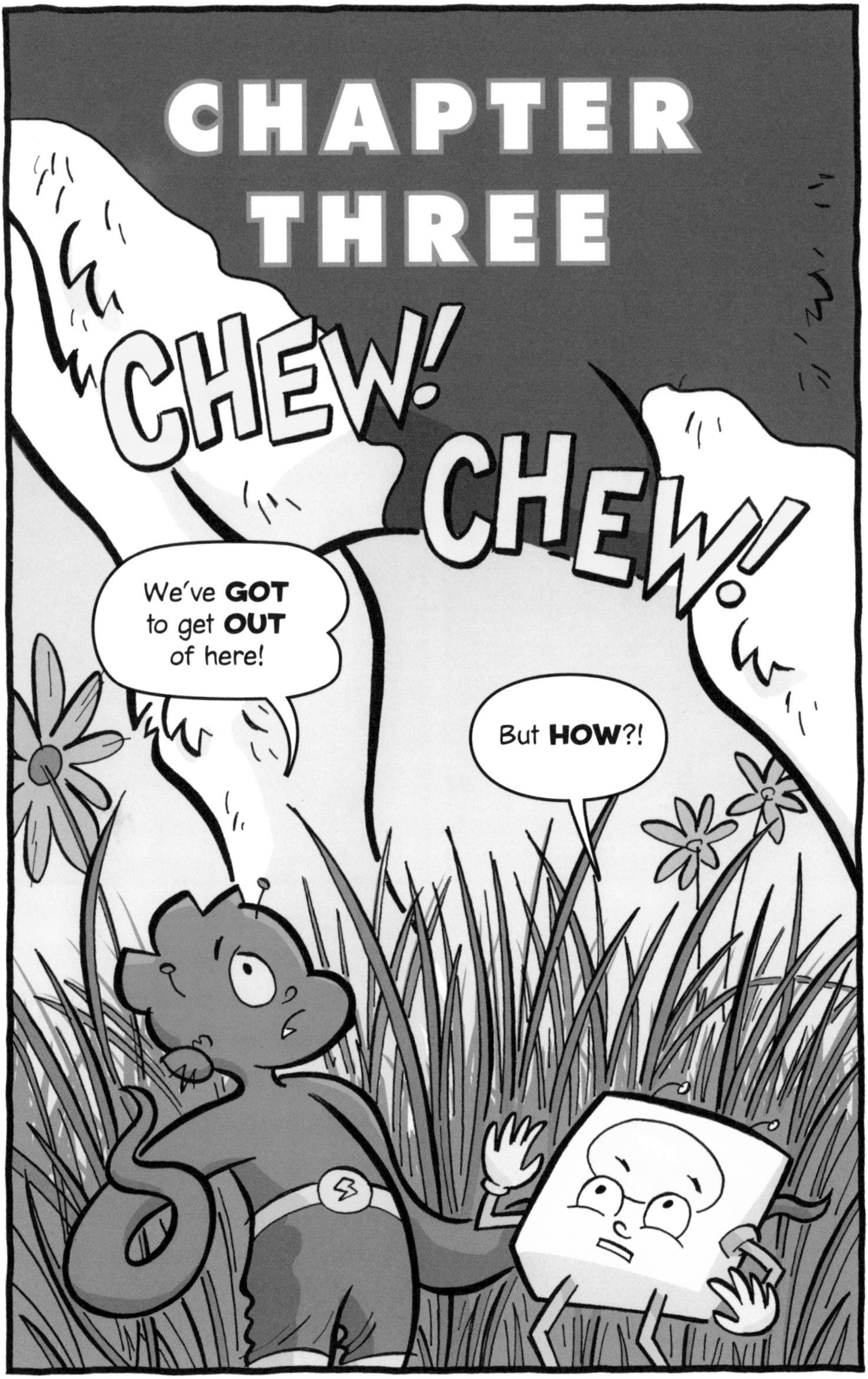
CHAPTER THREE
CHEW! CHEW!
We've **GOT** to get **OUT** of here!
But **HOW**?!

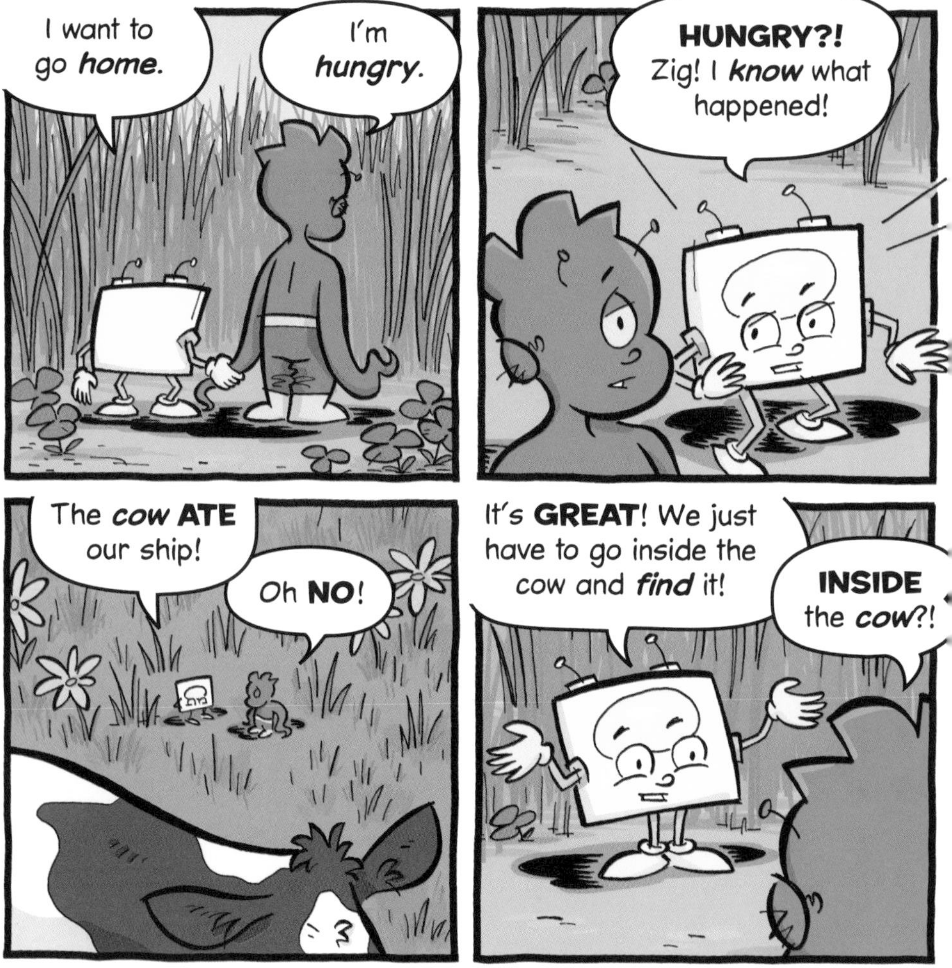
I want to go *home*.
I'm *hungry*.
HUNGRY?! Zig! I *know* what happened!
The *cow* **ATE** our ship!
Oh **NO**!
It's **GREAT**! We just have to go inside the cow and *find* it!
INSIDE the *cow*?!

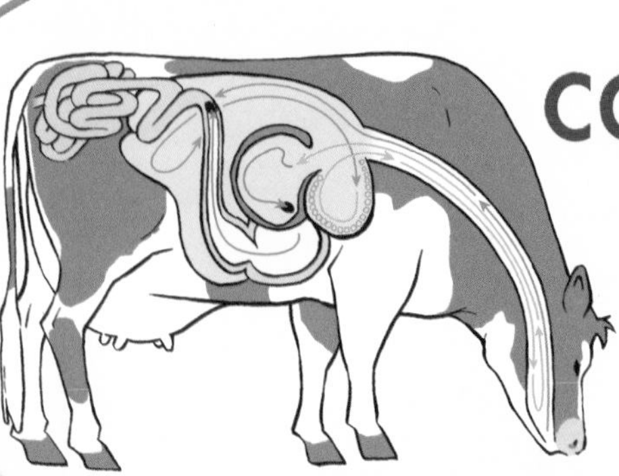

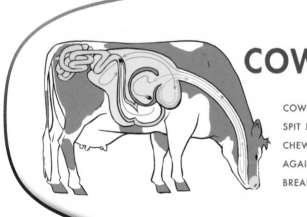

COW EATING

COWS SWALLOW GRASS, SPIT IT BACK UP, THEN CHEW IT AND SWALLOW IT AGAIN AND AGAIN TO HELP BREAK IT DOWN.

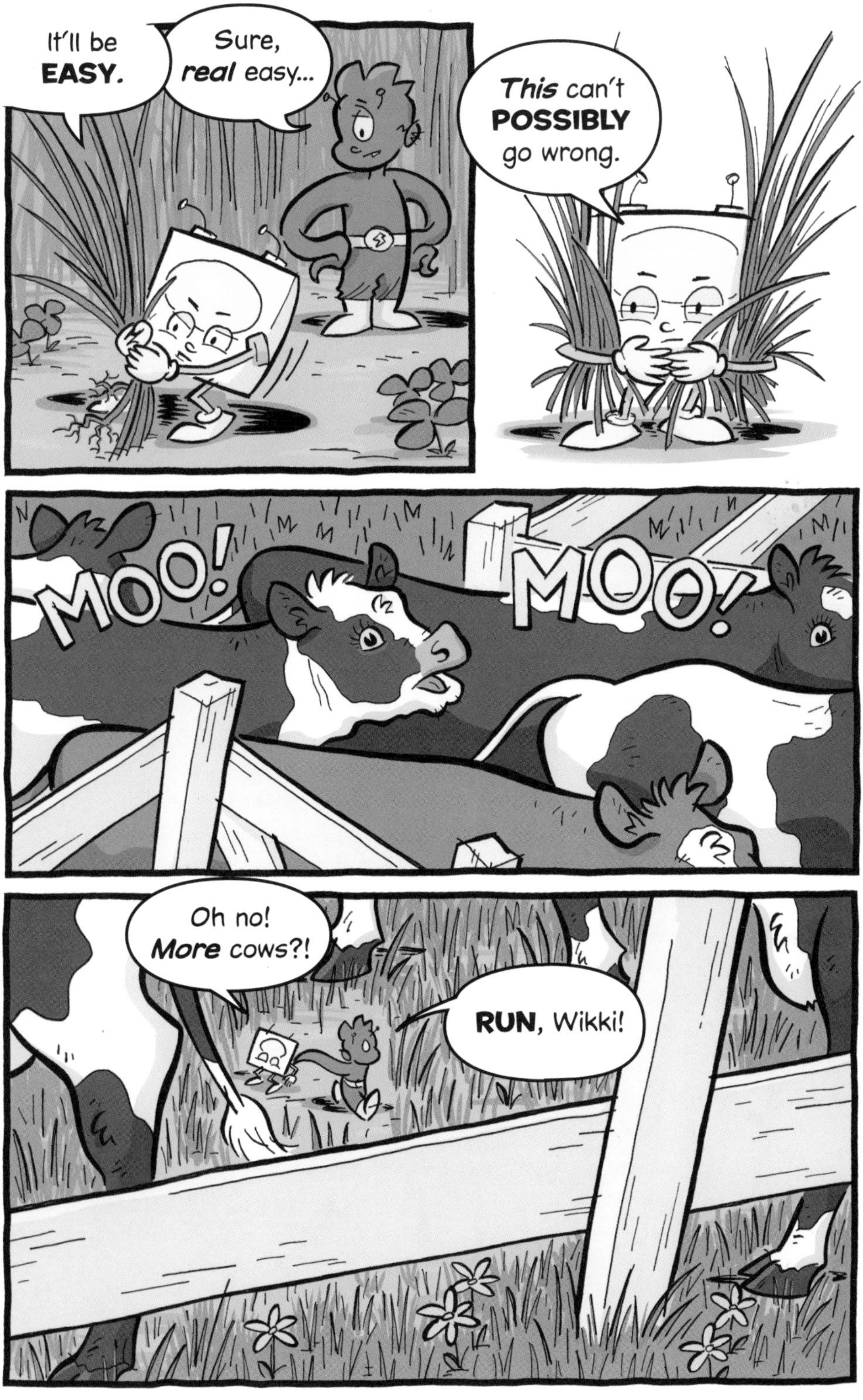
It'll be EASY.
Sure, real easy...
This can't POSSIBLY go wrong.
MOO!
MOO!
Oh no! More cows?!
RUN, Wikki!

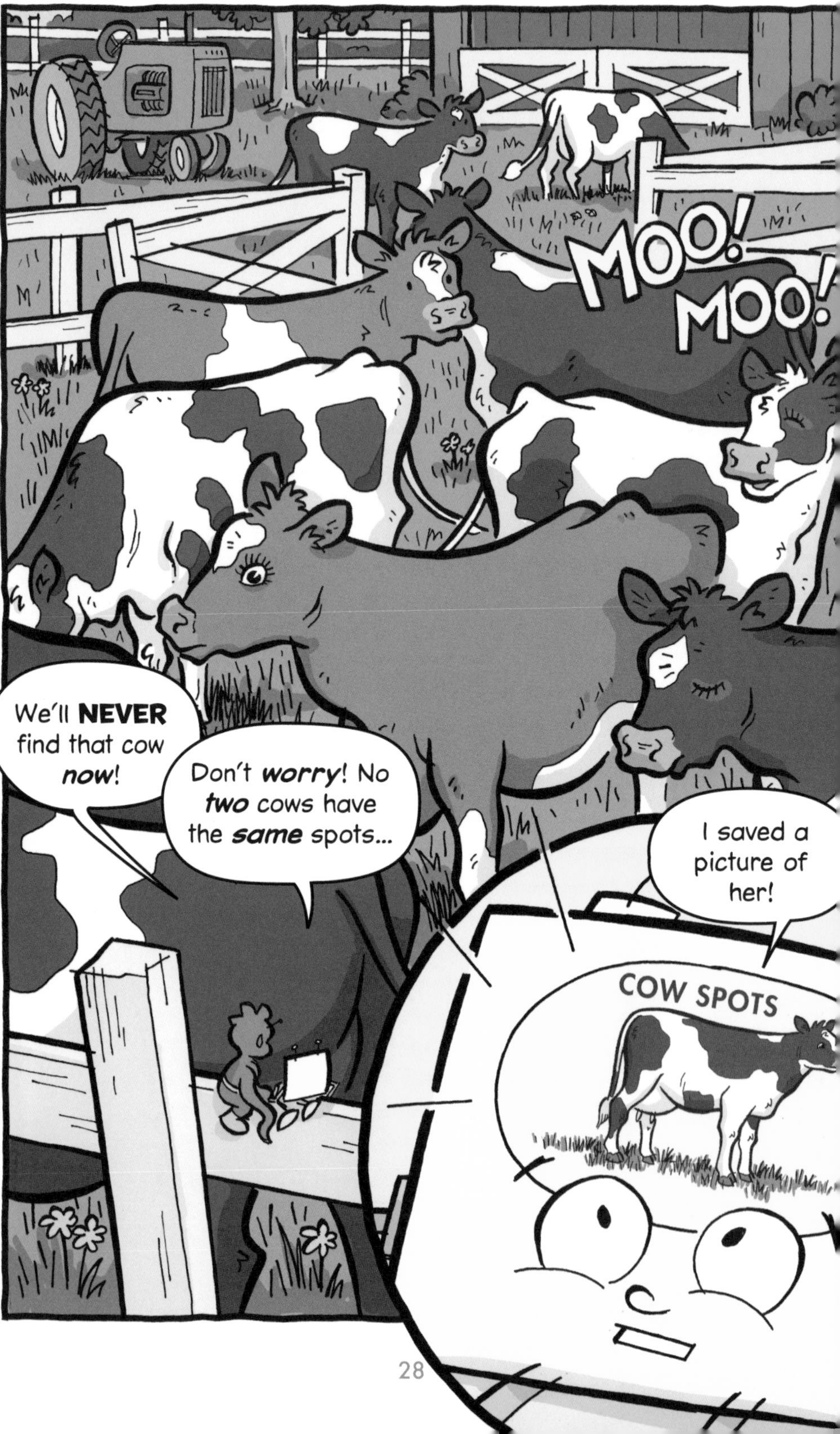
MOO!
MOO!
We'll **NEVER** find that cow *now*!
Don't *worry*! No *two* cows have the *same* spots...
I saved a picture of her!
COW SPOTS

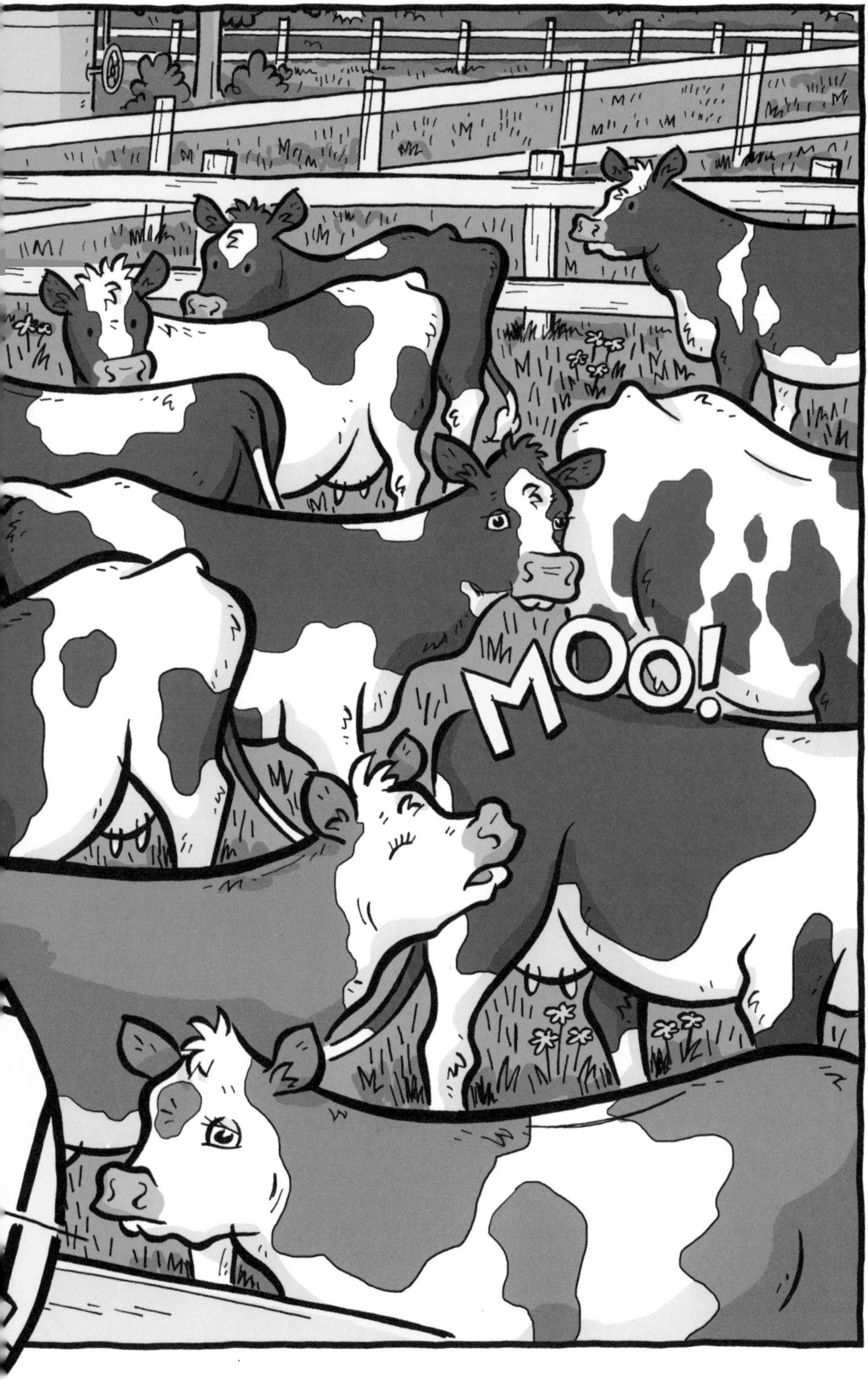
MOO!

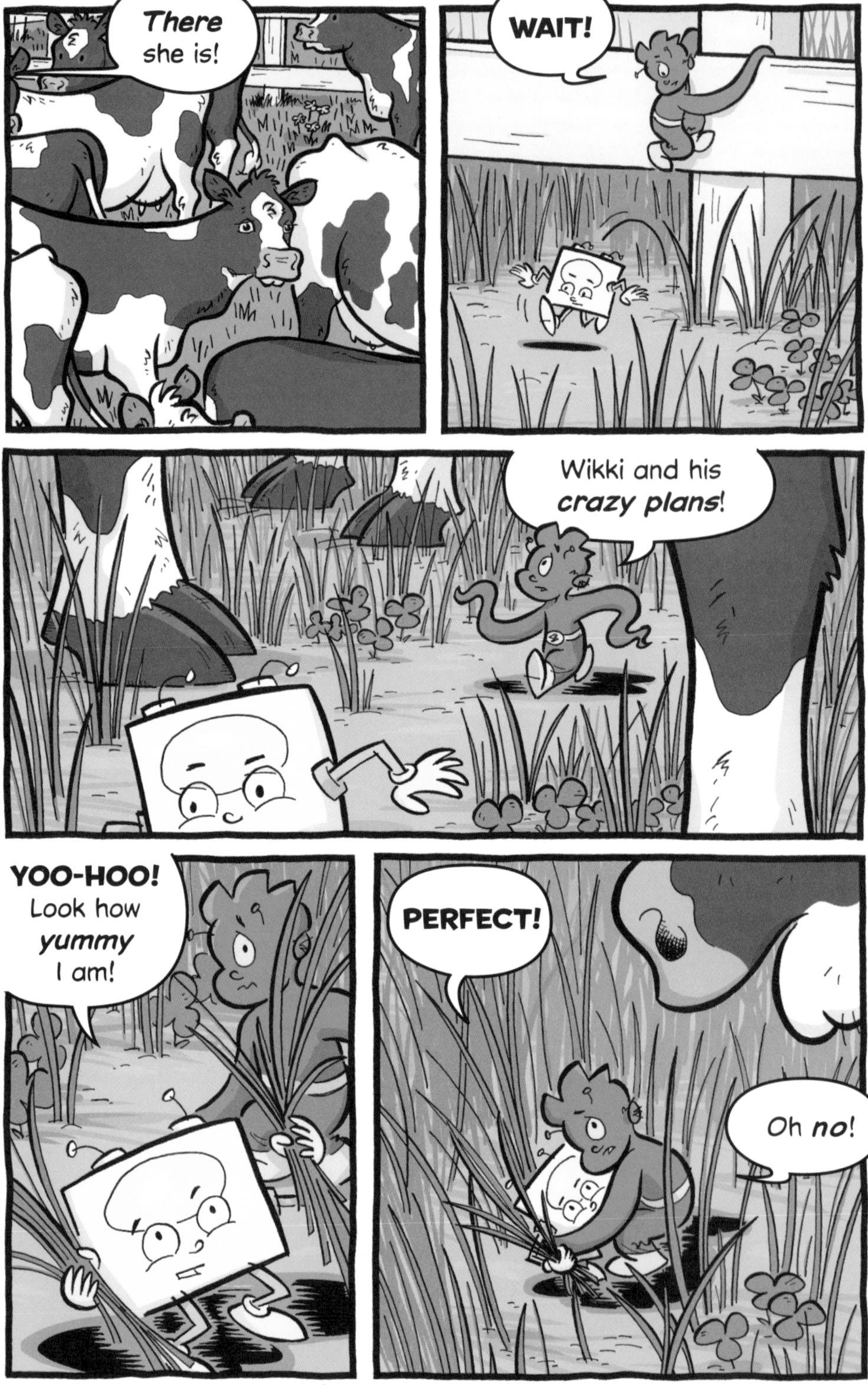
There she is!
WAIT!
Wikki and his crazy plans!
YOO-HOO! Look how yummy I am!
PERFECT!
Oh no!

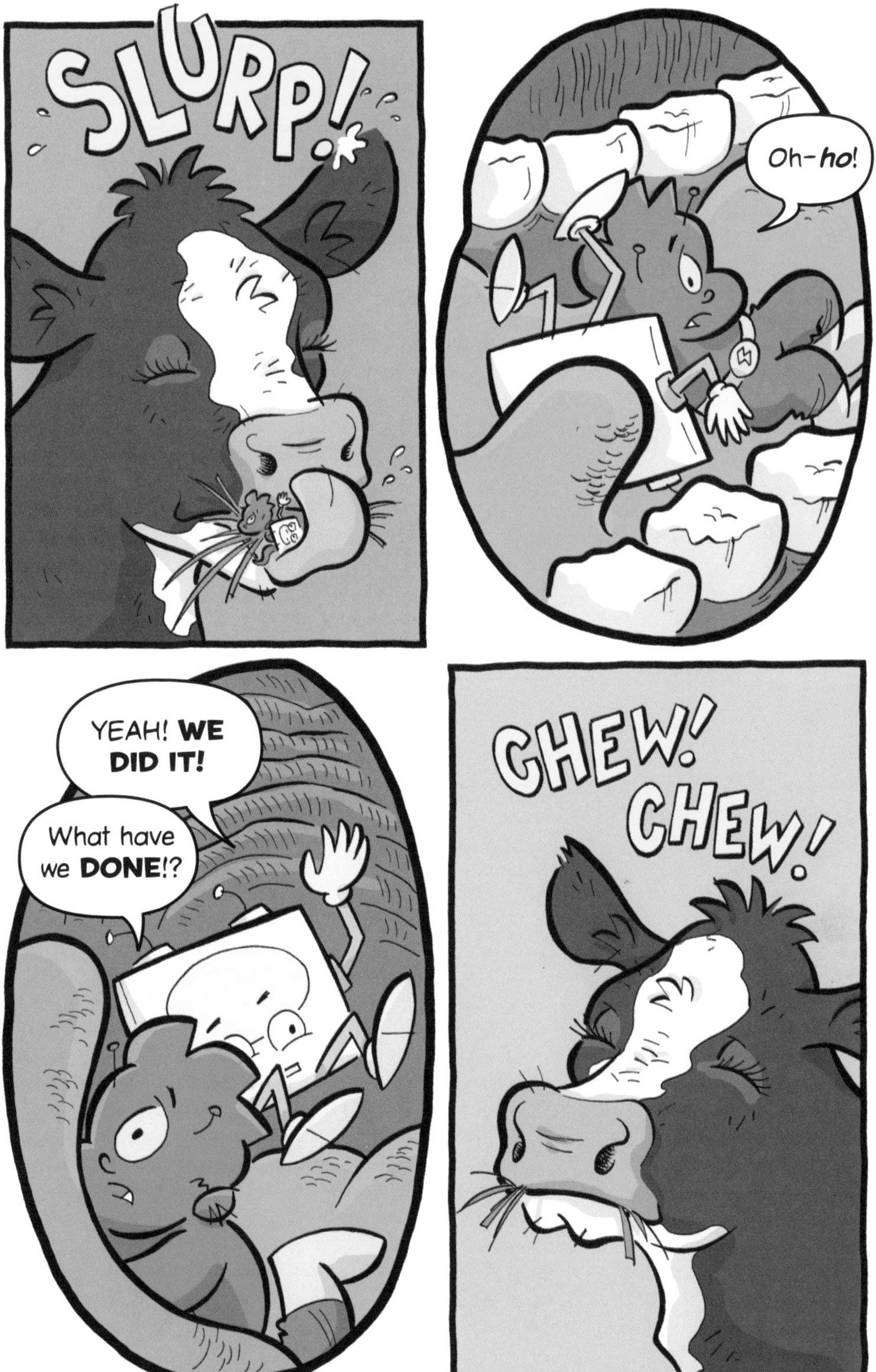

SLURP!
Oh-ho!
YEAH! WE DID IT!
What have we DONE!?
CHEW! CHEW!

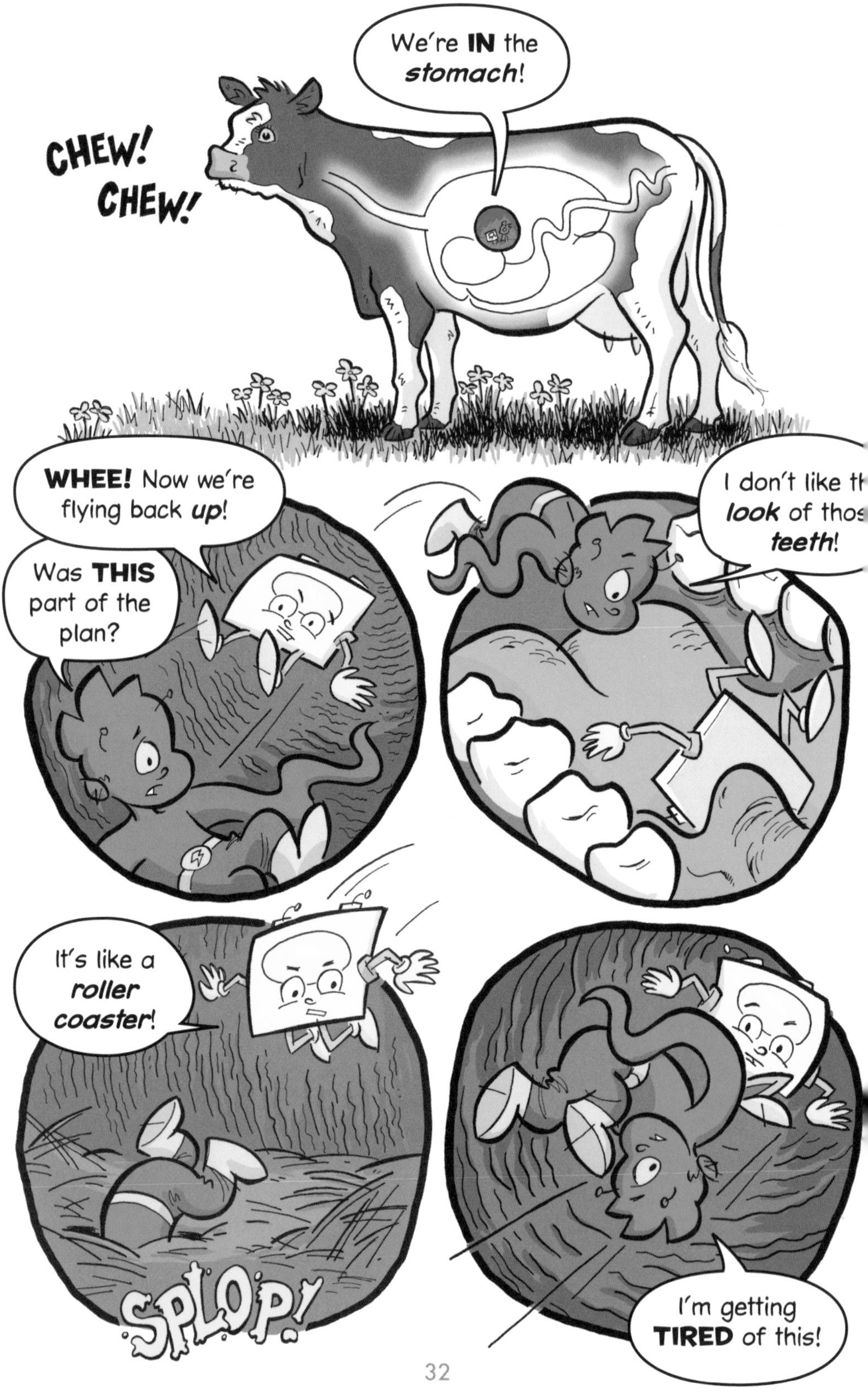
CHEW! CHEW!
We're **IN** the ***stomach***!
WHEE! Now we're flying back ***up***!
Was **THIS** part of the plan?
I don't like th
look of thos
teeth!
It's like a ***roller coaster***!
SPLOP!
I'm getting **TIRED** of this!

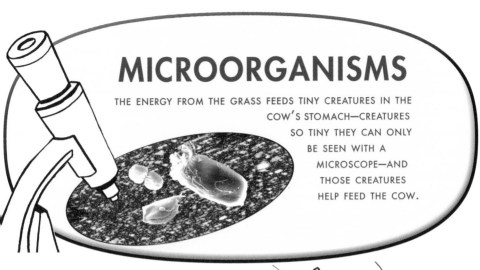

MICROORGANISMS

THE ENERGY FROM THE GRASS FEEDS TINY CREATURES IN THE COW'S STOMACH—CREATURES SO TINY THEY CAN ONLY BE SEEN WITH A MICROSCOPE—AND THOSE CREATURES HELP FEED THE COW.

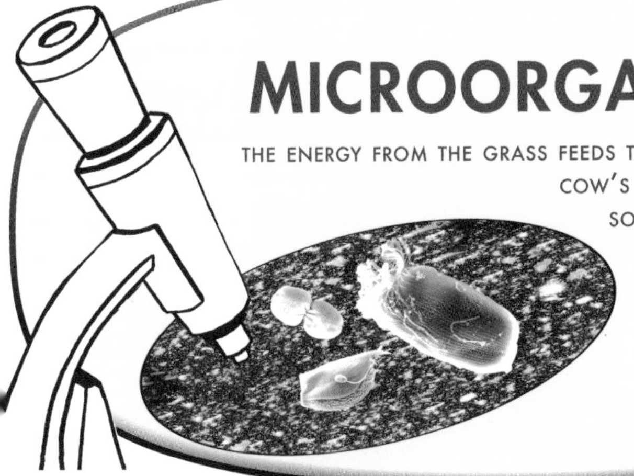

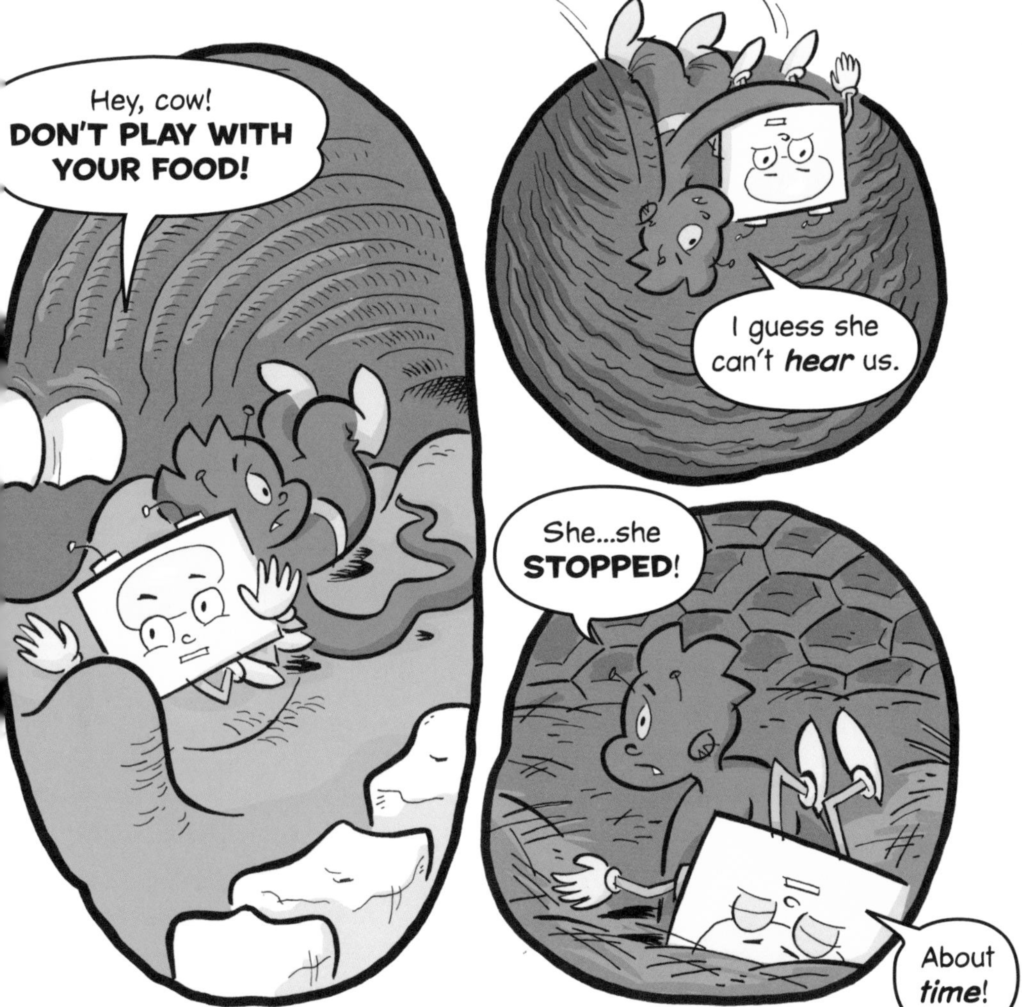

Hey, cow! **DON'T PLAY WITH YOUR FOOD!**
I guess she can't ***hear*** us.
She...she **STOPPED**!
About ***time***!

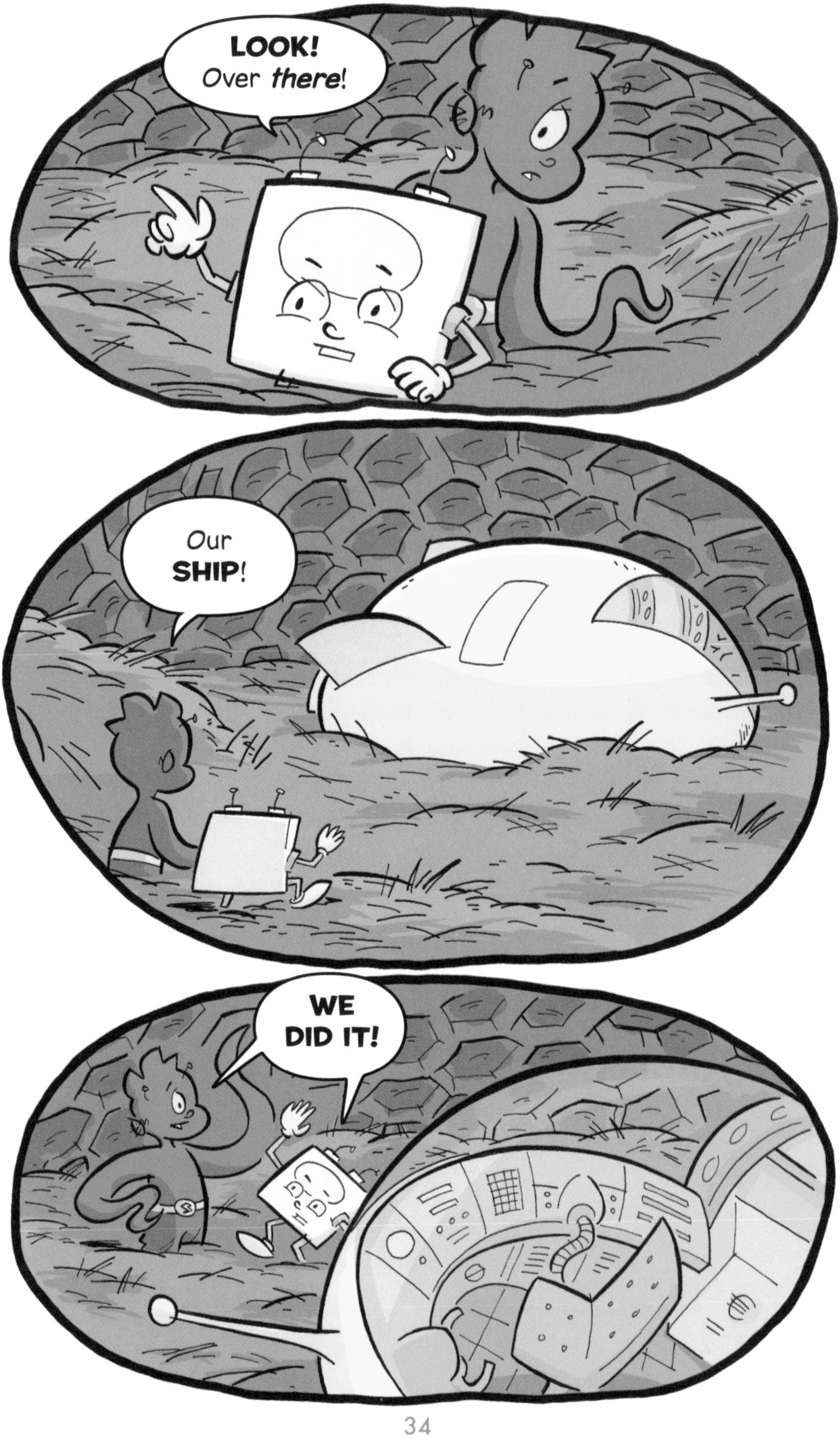
LOOK!
Over there!
Our SHIP!
WE DID IT!

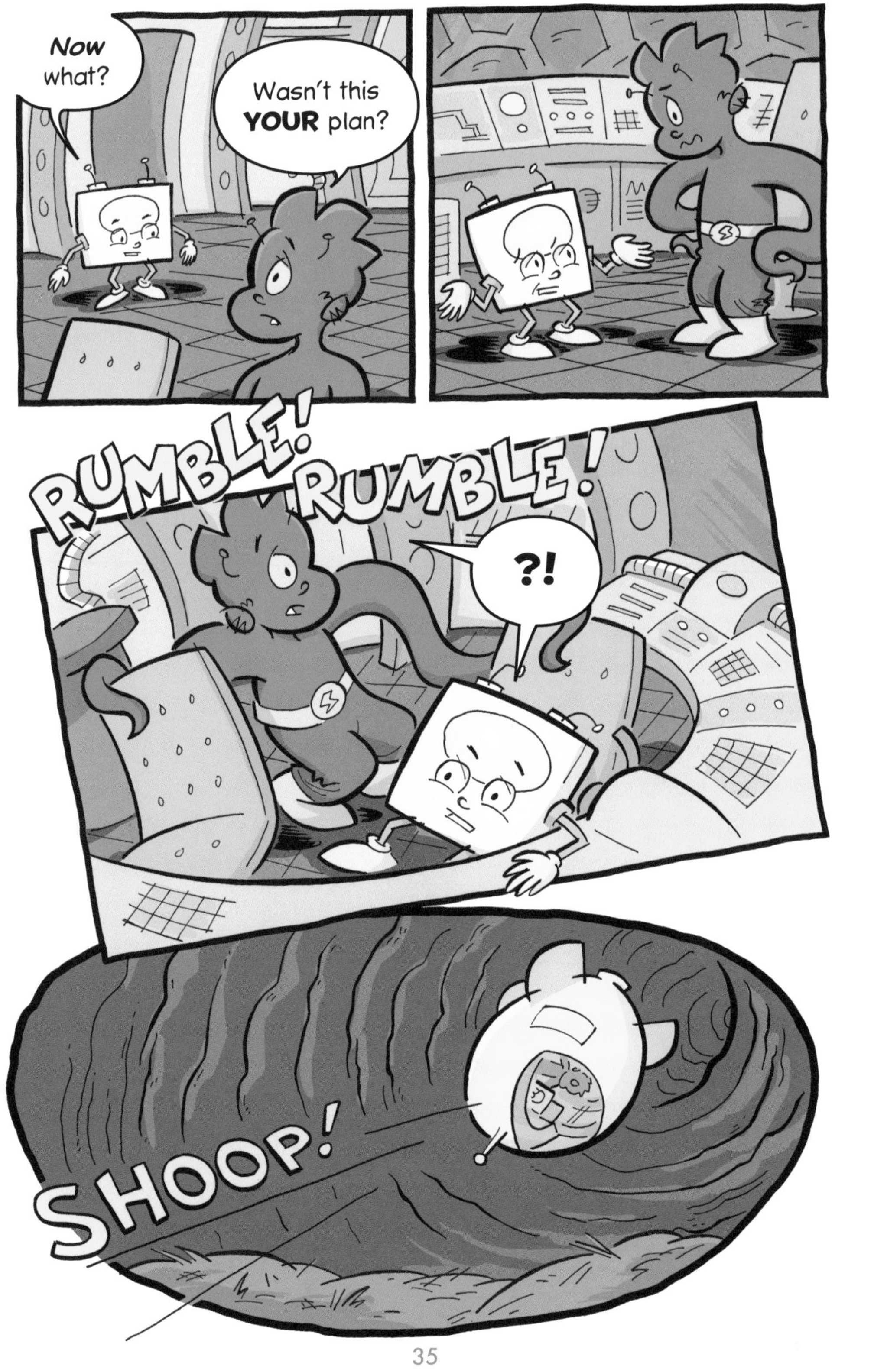
Now what?
Wasn't this YOUR plan?
RUMBLE! RUMBLE!
?!
SHOOP!

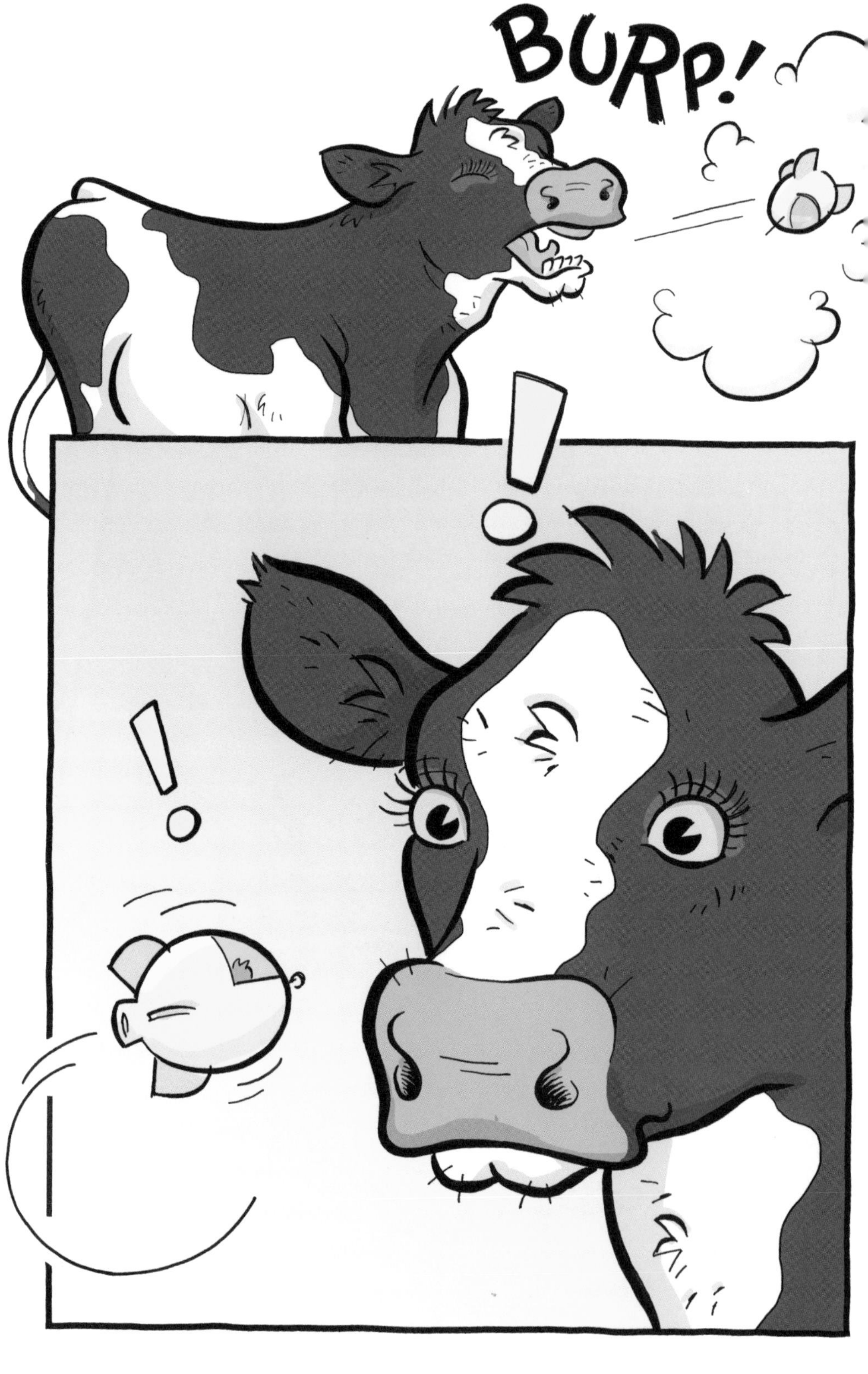
BURP!

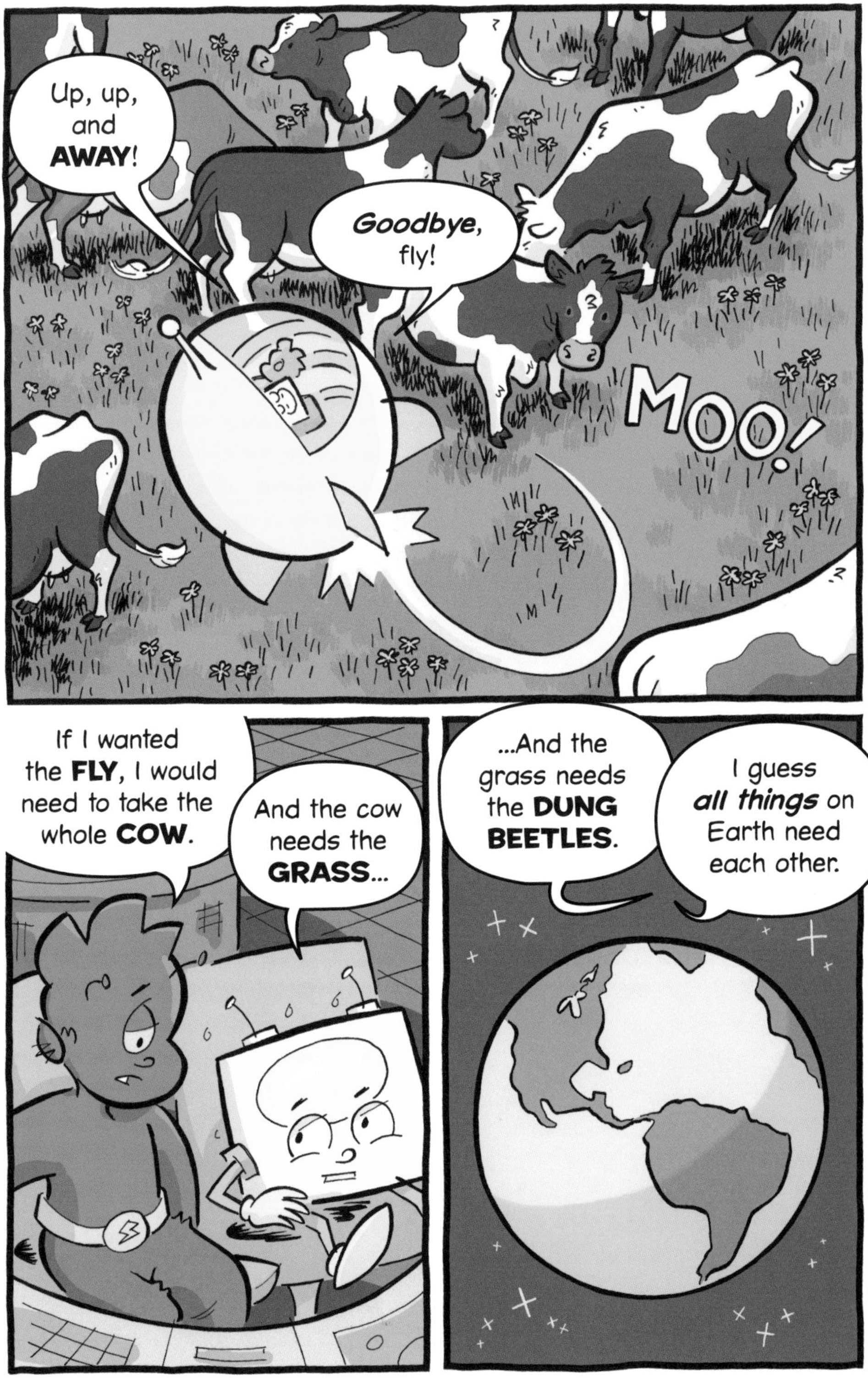
Up, up, and AWAY!
Goodbye, fly!
MOO!
If I wanted the FLY, I would need to take the whole COW.
And the cow needs the GRASS...
...And the grass needs the DUNG BEETLES.
I guess all things on Earth need each other.

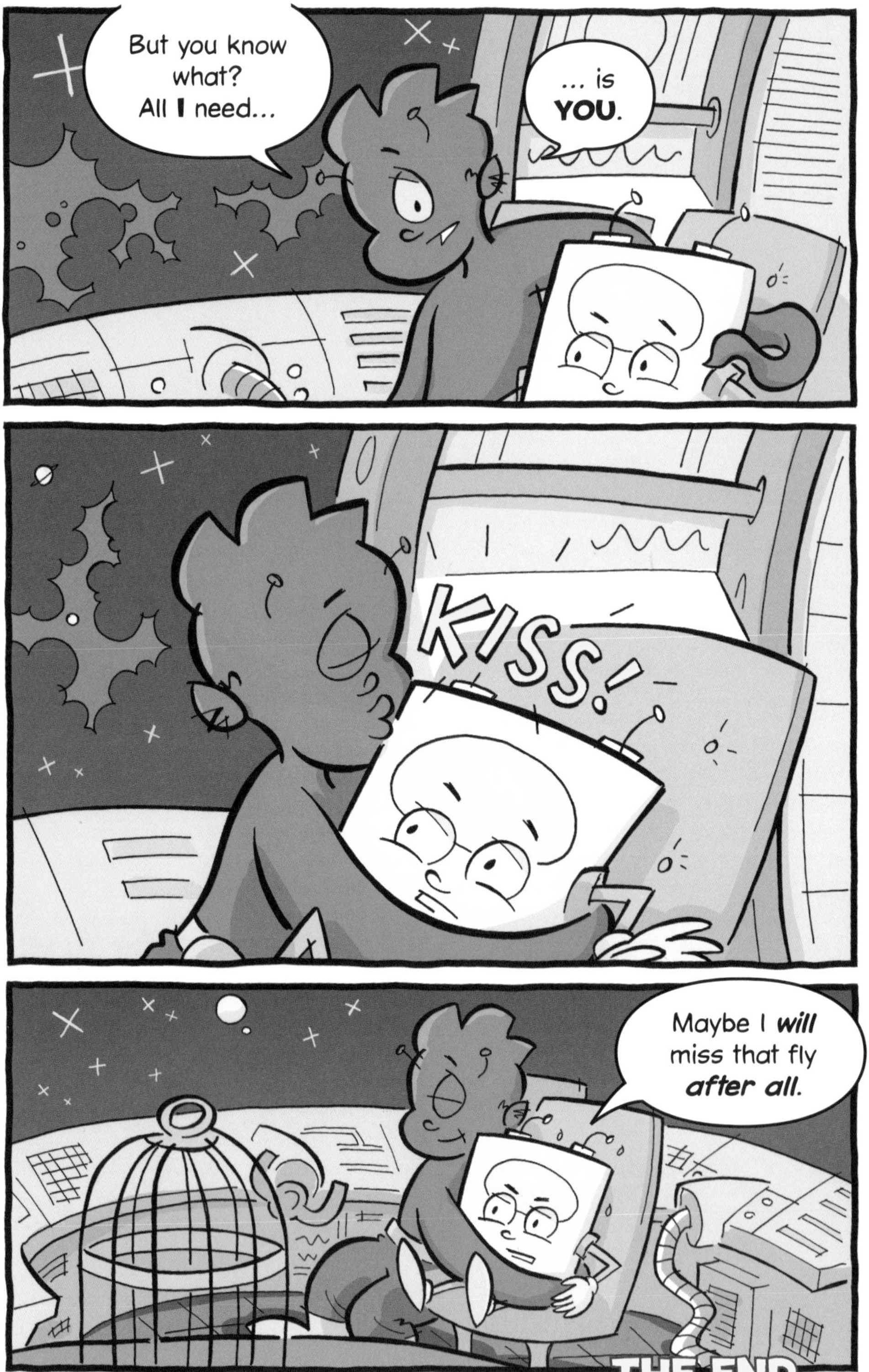
But you know what? All I need...
... is YOU.
KISS!
Maybe I will miss that fly after all.
THE END

ABOUT THE AUTHORS

NADJA SPIEGELMAN, who writes Zig and Wikki's adventures, likes cooking, writing, and decorating her apartment with furniture found on the street. She grew up in New York City, but loves going on vacation to the countryside. Once, when she was very young, a cow mistook her bright yellow dress for a flower and tried to eat her. She's still a little afraid of cows, but she'd like to learn how to milk one.

TRADE LOEFFLER, who draws Zig and Wikki, lives in Brooklyn, New York, with his wife, son, and their dog, Boo. Trade grew up in Livermore, California, the home of "the World's Fastest Rodeo," an event complete with bull riding and wild cow milking. Although he grew up in a "cow town," Trade has never considered himself a cowboy—even though he does own two pairs of cowboy boots.

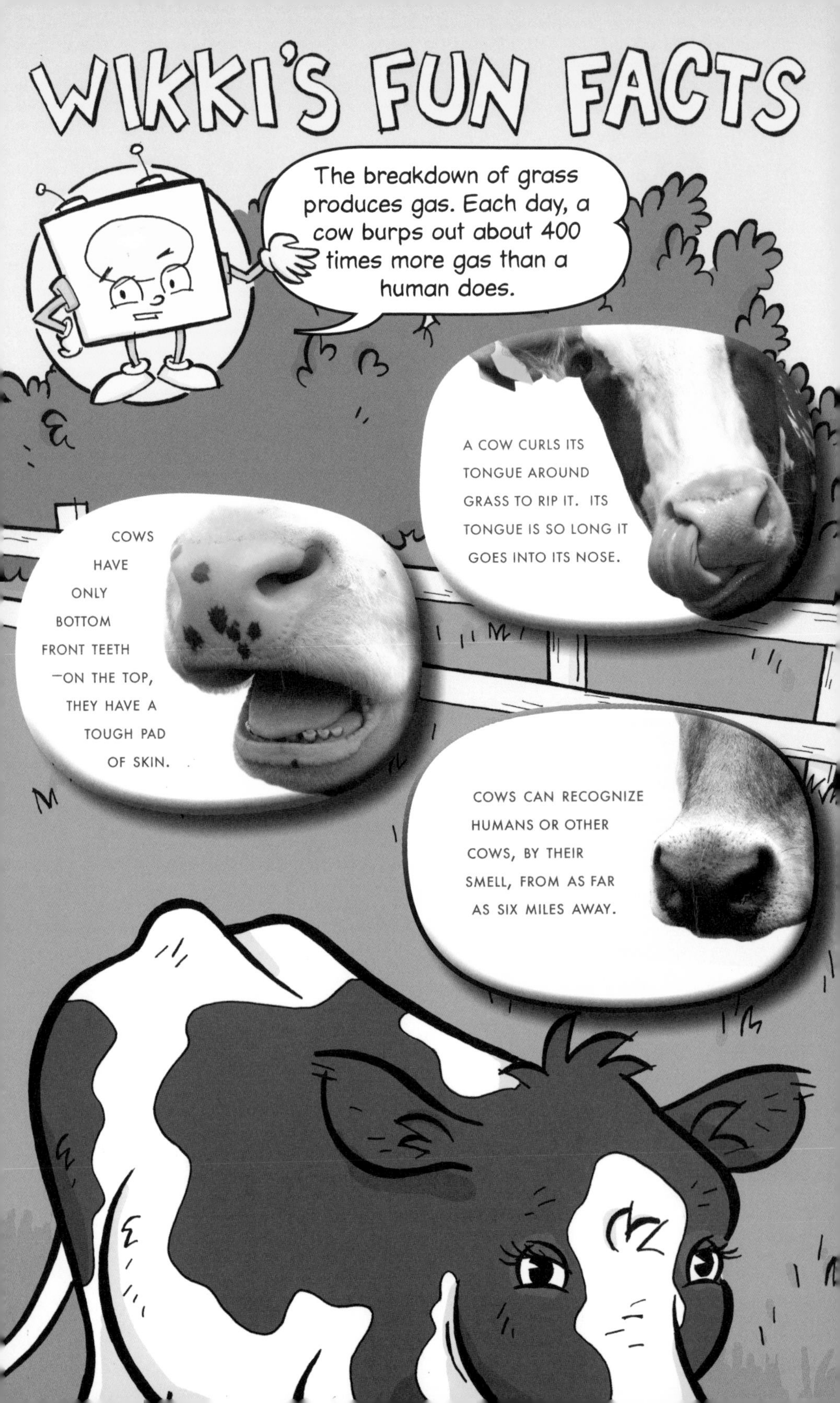
WIKKI'S FUN FACTS
The breakdown of grass produces gas. Each day, a cow burps out about 400 times more gas than a human does.
A COW CURLS ITS TONGUE AROUND GRASS TO RIP IT. ITS TONGUE IS SO LONG IT GOES INTO ITS NOSE.
COWS HAVE ONLY BOTTOM FRONT TEETH —ON THE TOP, THEY HAVE A TOUGH PAD OF SKIN.
COWS CAN RECOGNIZE HUMANS OR OTHER COWS, BY THEIR SMELL, FROM AS FAR AS SIX MILES AWAY.

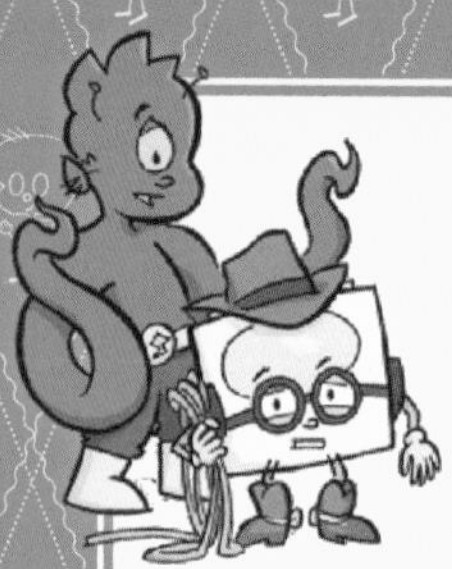

TIPS FOR PARENTS AND TEACHERS:

HOW TO READ COMICS WITH KIDS

Kids **love** comics! They are naturally drawn to the details in the pictures, which make them want to read the words. Comics beg for repeated readings and let both emerging and reluctant readers enjoy complex stories with a rich vocabulary. But since comics have their own grammar, here are a few tips for reading them with kids:

GUIDE YOUNG READERS: Use your finger to show your place in the text, but keep it at the bottom of the speaking character so it doesn't hide the very important facial expressions.

HAM IT UP! Think of the comic book story as a play and don't hesitate to read with expression and intonation. Assign parts or get kids to supply the sound effects, a great way to reinforce phonics skills.

LET THEM GUESS. Comics provide lots of context for the words, so emerging readers can make informed guesses. Like jigsaw puzzles, comics ask readers to make connections, so check a young audience's understanding by asking "What's this character thinking?" (but don't be surprised if a kid finds some of the comics' subtle details faster than you).

TALK ABOUT THE PICTURES. Point out how the artist paces the story with pauses (silent panels) or speeded-up action (a burst of short panels). Discuss how the size and shape of the panels carry meaning.

ABOVE ALL, ENJOY! There is of course never one right way to read, so go for the shared pleasure. Once children make the story happen in their imagination, they have discovered the thrill of reading, and you won't be able to stop them. At that point, just go get them more books, and more comics.

WWW.TOON-BOOKS.COM

SEE OUR FREE ONLINE CARTOON MAKERS,
LESSON PLANS, AND MUCH MORE

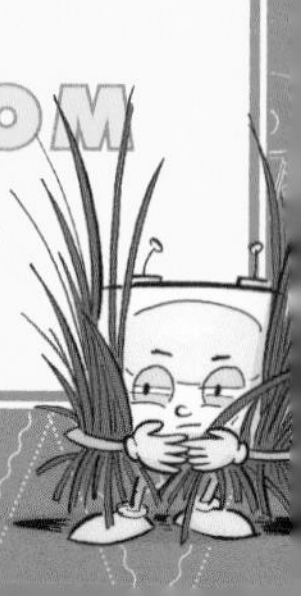